IMPROVING HEALTH AND
WELFARE WORK
WITH FAMILIES IN POVERTY

A Handbook

Also published by Open University Press:

POVERTY AND HEALTH: Working with Families
Clare Blackburn

This book is concerned with the relationship between poverty and health – and in particular the health of families with young children. A growing body of research has pointed to the way poverty affects the health of those who experience it. This has underlined the need for those who work with families to understand and respond more effectively to the health and welfare needs that poverty creates. Whilst a rich source of material on poverty and family health exists, it has not been readily available to health and welfare workers. This book brings together this material and makes it accessible to those who are concerned about the health of families with young children. Drawing on a wide range of disciplines it uses both 'hard' and 'soft' data in the acknowledgement that we need not only facts and figures but first hand accounts if we are to understand how poverty impacts on family health and family life.

0-335-09734-0 (paperback)
0-335-09735-9 (hardback)

CHILD HEALTH MATTERS: Caring for Children in the Community
Sally Wyke and Jenny Hewison (eds)

0-335-09393-0 (paperback)
0-335-09394-9 (hardback)

MEASURING HEALTH: A Review of Quality of Life Measurement Scales
Ann Bowling

0-335-15435-2 (paperback)
0-335-15436-0 (hardback)

CARING FOR PEOPLE
Jenny Rogers

0-335-09429-5 (paperback)
0-335-09430-9 (hardback)

IMPROVING HEALTH AND WELFARE WORK WITH FAMILIES IN POVERTY

A Handbook

Clare Blackburn

OPEN UNIVERSITY PRESS

Buckingham • Philadelphia

Open University Press
Celtic Court
22 Ballmoor
Buckingham
MK18 1XW

and
1900 Frost Road, Suite 101,
Bristol, PA 19007, USA

First Published 1992

A catalogue record of this book is available from the British Library.

Library of Congress Cataloging-in-Publication Data

Blackburn, Clare, 1957 –
Improving health and welfare work with families in poverty : a handbook / by Clare Blackburn.

p. cm.

Includes bibliographical references and index.

ISBN 0-335-09732-4 (pbk.)

1. Poverty--Health aspects--Handbooks, manuals, etc.   2. Poor--Health and hygiene--Handbooks, manuals, etc.   3. Medical social work--Handbooks, manuals, etc.
4. Social service--Team work--Handbooks, manuals, etc.   I. Title.

RA418.5.P6B52   1992
362. 1'0452 – dc20   91-46006
                                                                                 CIP

Printed in Great Britain by
St Edmundsbury Press,
Bury St Edmunds, Suffolk.

CONTENTS

Acknowledgements

I would like to express my thanks to a number of people. Foremost, I would like to thank Hilary Graham and Norma Baldwin, whose advice has been invaluable and without whose support this handbook would not have been possible. Thanks are also due to Meg Bond and Ruth Elkan who read drafts and helped with copy-editing. Members of the Development and Evaluation Group – Dorit Braun, Jill Blackshaw, Ruby Dillon, Ann James, Gwen Mellon, Heather Page and Kamlesh Sharman – helped with the development of ideas and provided feedback. Lyn Carruthers, Norma Baldwin, Kate Billingham and Ann Rowe kindly gave up their time to write up their practice experiences. Thanks also to Pete Hyde, whose eye for layout and design has compensated for my lack of imagination. Finally, I would like to express my thanks to the Health Promotion Research Trust who funded the development of this handbook, and the complementary text *Poverty and Health: Working with Families*. The ideas expressed in this handbook, and any deficiencies, are those of the author and not necessarily those of the Health Promotion Research Trust or those who provided help and support.

Figures 2.1 and 2.3 are reproduced with the permission of the Controller, HMSO and are subject to Crown copyright. Table 3.1 is reproduced with the kind permission of Child Poverty Action Group from their publication 'The Costs of a Child'. This publication is available from Child Poverty Action Group, 1–5 Bath Street, London EC1V 9PY, price £3.50.

List of Abbreviations

CPN: Community psychiatric nurse
DoE: Department of Employment
GP: General practitioner
HA: Health authority
HV: Health visitor
LA: Local authority
OPCS: Office of Population, Censuses and Surveys
SSD: Social Services Department
UK: United Kingdom

INTRODUCING THE TEAM TRAINING HANDBOOK

This team training handbook is concerned with the implications of family poverty for health and welfare practice. It considers issues and questions that health and welfare workers face daily in their work with families in poverty. It focuses on the health and welfare of one particular kind of family: families with dependent children.

Who is the Team Training Handbook For?

Can you and the team you work with answer the following questions?

- How many families in poverty are there in your neighbourhood?
- How many local children are growing up in conditions of poverty?
- Where are families in poverty located in the neighbourhood?
- Which groups are most at risk of poverty?
- What services are available for families in poverty?
- What are the income, housing, health, childcare and social support needs of local families?
- How does poverty affect the physical and mental health of local families, and shape the choices they make?
- Can you explain the complex links between poverty and ill-health?

If you cannot answer all these questions then you and your team need this team training handbook!

This team training handbook is designed for teams of health and welfare practitioners who work with families with dependent children:

✓ Health visiting and community nursing teams
✓ Social work teams
✓ Nursery workers
✓ Community workers
✓ Community education teams
✓ Other community-based teams from both the statutory and voluntary sectors

While the handbook is directed at health and welfare teams, it may also be a useful resource to other groups, including:

- Workers who do not have the opportunity to use the materials with a team but who wish to examine poverty and poor health as an issue for their individual work
- Staff development officers and trainers
- Staff who teach qualifying and post-qualifying courses in social work, community nursing, and community work
- Students on qualifying and post-qualifying health and welfare courses

Why a Team Training Handbook on Poverty and Health?

• **Poverty levels among families with children have increased substantially over the last decade.** Between 1979 and 1987 the number of families with children in poverty (with incomes below 50 per cent of average income) increased from 2.8 million to 5.5 million. In 1987, families with children were the largest single group in poverty, making up 53 per cent of all people in poverty.

• **Poverty amongst families reflects the wider social divisions of 'race', social class and gender.** For some people, their social position renders them at high risk of poverty. Families with heads of households who are unemployed or who work in the less secure sectors of the labour market, families headed by lone mothers, Black and minority ethnic families, and families with people with disabilities are all disproportionately represented amongst those in poverty.

• **The evidence suggests that poverty needs to be a central concern of health and welfare work.** Yet, health and welfare practice is rarely based on a sound knowledge of the effects of poverty on family life and family health. There is a two-way relationship between health and welfare work, on the one hand, and family poverty on the other:

* *The effects of poverty on family health and well-being lead many families to become users of health and welfare services.* Poor families are heavy users of services and substantial proportions of resources are directly and indirectly absorbed by them.

* *The nature and style of health and welfare interventions have an influence on how families experience poverty and poverty-related problems.* When services are flexible and responsive, they can help families cope with and avoid the worst elements of poverty. They can provide a challenge to policy-makers to develop strategies that reduce poverty. When services are inflexible or fail to acknowledge poverty as an issue for practice, they can serve to compound the negative experience of poverty on family life and family health.

• **The Children Act (Section 17) requires local authorities to safeguard and promote the welfare of children within their area by providing a range and level of services appropriate to those children's needs.** To carry out these responsibilities, fieldworkers will need to assess the needs of children in poverty and their families. Many teams will need to

develop or extend community profiling activities. This handbook will help teams to increase their awareness of how poverty affects the health and well-being of children and families and increase their skill to assess and meet their needs.

Reflecting the above four factors, this handbook has been written for fieldworkers who want to place poverty on the central agenda of fieldwork practice. Health and welfare workers have an important role to play in the development of practice which takes account of poverty and promotes anti-poverty strategies. The materials in this handbook seek to encourage and enable workers to take on this role.

Philosophy of the Handbook

A structural explanation of poverty underlies the materials in this handbook. Poverty is seen as the consequence of social and economic inequalities which reduce the access of some groups to income and essential material and social resources, rather than simply the consequence of the personal characteristics, behaviour, attitudes or knowledge levels of individuals.

The handbook uses a structural explanation to account for the close link between poverty and poor health. The materials reflect the view that the major effects of poverty on health stem from the social and economic environment in which families live, and the everyday world within which they care for families within the home. Poverty affects health by reducing access to essential material and social resources for health and well-being. Poverty is also seen to affect health indirectly by shaping family health choices.

This handbook is underpinned by the assumption that the material consequences of poverty are such that individualised explanations cannot account for the links between poverty and ill health.

Key Features of the Team Training Handbook

• **The team training handbook brings staff development and training to the fieldwork team.** These materials are designed to be used 'in situ' by agencies within their neighbourhood bases. In recent years, new demands on health and welfare workers, coupled with cuts in resources, have made it increasingly difficult for staff to leave the field to participate in staff development and training. The content and format of the materials recognise these constraints on training.

• **This team training handbook provides a new form of staff development and training.** Traditional approaches to staff development and training provide limited opportunities for neighbourhood workers to explore practice issues **together as a team.** Teams need to engage in specific learning that enhances their ability to function as a task group. Workers need the opportunity to look at how they relate to each other and to the community in which they work, and to engage together in a process of planned change. Taking staff development to the whole team provides an opportunity to do this. Research studies indicate that many fieldworkers fail to see poverty, and the health problems associated with it, as central to their everyday work with families. Putting poverty on the central agenda of health and welfare work requires teams to examine together the issue and what it means for their collective and individual practice.

• **The team training handbook is a team resource, rather than a trainer's resource.** It is written to be used by teams themselves and does not rely on a trainer to provide background information or facilitate the learning process. This is in recognition that not all teams have easy access to a trainer or staff development officer. The team training handbook is content- as well as process-driven: it provides key information as well as activities that will assist workers to develop responsive support strategies for families in poverty.

• **The team training handbook highlights the importance of inter-agency collaboration as a major issue for health and welfare practice.** Changes to the structure and organisation of health and welfare services in the last decade have brought about the need for more integrative and collaborative methods of service delivery. Yet, fieldwork experience suggests that collaborative work across the health and welfare field is infrequent and fragmented. Materials which focus on inter-agency team work can promote greater collaboration between health and welfare agencies.

What Does the Team Training Handbook Do?

• **'Improving Health and Welfare Work with Families in Poverty' provides key information, sets of guide-lines, and activities.** Together these enable workers to move through the process of learning and planning.

• **The team training handbook focuses on the processes that teams of workers need to go through to build responsive strategies rather than on prescribing outcomes.** This approach has been adopted for two reasons. First, teams start from different points, face different circumstances and have different roles. Secondly, teams need to work out their own plans, priorities and solutions with local communities and within and across agencies rather than use 'textbook' solutions or prescribed blue-prints for practice.

• **The materials provide a step-by-step approach to learning and planning around problems and issues of poverty.** They identify the key stages of planning and action for teams to work through. The key stages are the same for all teams, although the outcomes will be different, depending on local needs and circumstances and the roles of individual neighbourhood teams. The key stages are identified in the flow chart below. Although the team training handbook treats each stage separately to assist learning, you will find that, in reality, they are interlinked. For example, you will find that you are still developing your understanding of poverty issues while you are working through the stage of setting goals for practice.

Key Stages

Clarifying the issues and organising the process of team training

Examining attitudes to and beliefs about poverty

Developing an understanding of poverty and its effects on health

Making an assessment of local family poverty

Evaluating family   Setting goals
support strategies   for practice

Engaging with families in poverty

The bottom section of the flow chart denotes a cyclical process. Although the team training handbook ends with the evaluation stage of learning and planning, you should not end your work here! Your evaluation will highlight the need for new information and a continuous reformulation of goals and action plans.

> **Each section of the team training handbook examines one of these key stages of learning and planning around poverty and family health.**

Section 1: will help your team to consider why poverty is an issue for you, and come to some agreement about how you will organise the learning and planning process.

Section 2: provides a framework for you to examine how poverty is defined and explained, and an opportunity for you to look at how views about poverty, including your own, shape fieldwork practice with families.

Section 3: helps you to build up your knowledge of family poverty. It examines what the experience of poverty means for family life and looks at the complex links between income and family health.

Section 4: looks at how poverty and its impact on families can be assessed. It looks at the value of building local poverty profiles, and provides sets of guidelines for compiling and analysing them.

Section 5: examines the process of planning for change. It provides a framework for thinking about appropriate roles and tasks for workers in family poverty work. This section then looks at how information from poverty profiles can be used to set goals and priorities for the team. It discusses some of the organisational factors that constrain goal-setting.

Section 6: discusses the process of engaging with families in poverty. It looks at the way in which different methods can be used to support families.

Section 7: looks at how you can begin to evaluate your work with families in poverty.

Section 8: provides a list of useful references and resources on family poverty.

What Sorts of Work Might Come Out of Using the Team Training Handbook?

- Schemes to increase neighbourhood support for isolated families;
- Welfare rights sessions attached to child health clinics;
- Consumer participation in service planning;
- Food co-operatives and credit unions;
- Better childcare facilities.

Timescale for Using the Handbook

Sections	Activities	Length of each activity	Total time for completing section
Section 1	1A 1B	1 hour 1 hour	2 hours (1 session)
Section 2	2A 2B	1 hour 2 hours	3 hours (1 session)
Section 3	3A 3B	90 mins 90 mins	3 hours (1 session)
Section 4	4A 4B 4C	3 hours 3 – 4 hours 1 hour	7 – 8 hours (2 x $\frac{1}{2}$ days)
Section 5	5A 5B	75 mins 2 x 3 hours	8 hours (2 x $\frac{1}{2}$ days)
Section 6	6A 6B 6C 6D	90 mins 3 hours 100 mins 1 hour	6 – 7 hours (3 sessions)
Section 7	7A 7B	2 hours 1 hour	3 hours (1 session)

The timings for sessions are only suggestions. You can have shorter sessions or collapse some of the sessions into full day or $\frac{1}{2}$ day sessions if you prefer.

USING THE
TEAM TRAINING HANDBOOK

Organisation of the Materials

The team training handbook is divided into eight main sections. The first seven sections relate to the key stages identified in the flow chart on page 4. Each section contains the following sub-sections:

- **An introductory page**, which describes the aims of the section, lists team activities and information sheets and gives some notes for a facilitator (who can be a member of the team)
- **Team activities and action points**
- **Information sheets** to use with the team activities
- **A summary and conclusion**
- **References and notes**

Suggestions for further reading are given for each section and brought together in section 8.

> There is a complementary book, by the same author, that can be used with this handbook:
>
> Blackburn, C. (1991). **Poverty and Health: Working with Families.** Buckingham, Open University Press.

The symbol ▮ in the text denotes that information links with an activity.

Using the Materials

✓ **You should work through each section in turn.** The sections follow a sequential order. The sections will help you to move progressively towards the development of flexible and responsive family support strategies.

✓ **Agree a timescale for the work.** Some groups may need to spend longer on some sections of the pack than other groups, depending on knowledge levels within the team and the relevance of each issue to the work of the team.

✓ **Agree how you will use the materials.** Section 1 of the team training handbook offers some guidelines and provides a framework for you to think about how you will deal with the issues that arise.

✓ **Make sure everyone has access to the materials.** To work as a group, the whole team needs to use the materials.

✓ **The relevant information sheets will need to be read before the group meets.** They provide base-line information for the session. Your facilitator should bring to the attention of the team which information sheets need to be read. You may need to do some further reading in some areas. Suggestions for further reading are given, along with a list of other resources in section 8.

✓ **Someone should take responsibility for, or facilitate, each session.** Your group should discuss who is the most appropriate person/persons to do this. Some groups may prefer to nominate one person to take responsibility for all the sessions, while others may prefer to rotate the responsibility around the group.

Facilitator's Role

The term 'facilitator' describes the person who takes responsibility for a session or a series of sessions. As the materials reflect the fact that not all teams have access to a tutor or staff development officer, they do not assume that the facilitator has extensive training skills. However, facilitators should have some understanding of group work processes and some experience of collaborative and participatory methods of learning and planning.

The facilitator's role in this team training handbook is not that of a tutor or training officer who brings extensive knowledge of the issues to the sessions or who may decide the content of each session. The role of the facilitator is to ensure that the group learning process occurs. Below is a list of the facilitator's main responsibilities.

RESPONSIBILITIES OF THE FACILITATOR

- Ensure that all group members have access to the materials before and during a session;
- Start and end the sessions;
- Chair discussions;
- Ensure that all group members abide by the group's rules or contract (see section 1);
- Ensure that all group members have the opportunity to contribute their knowledge and experience on an equal basis;
- Ensure that all contributions are valued;
- Move the group through the learning materials;
- Provide a structure for feedback for the group;
- Ensure that group members are briefed of any work to be done before or after a session.

Definitions of Key Terms

- **'Family'** is used to describe a group of individuals who live together and use the same household resources. The term therefore refers to a social grouping of people rather than a natural or biological grouping. This is in recognition that there are many different family structures and forms of family life and that no one family type is preferable to others.

- **'Black'** is used to refer to people of African Caribbean and Asian descent. It is used to portray a common unity that is forged out of the experience of racism in British society. The term is used in the belief that it is one commonly used by Black people themselves, although this may change over time. Black is spelt with a capital letter to denote that the term refers to the social and political aspects of being Black rather than the colour of people's skin. By using the term Black the author does not wish to deny the diversity of cultures and ethnicities that together make up Britain's Black population.

- **'Minority ethnic'** refers to groups who are not necessarily Black, but who, like Black people, are in a minority in a numerical sense, and in the sense that they have minimal power in comparison to the majority ethnic group. When reading this term it should be borne in mind that the term refers to groups that each have their own cultural identity, history and way of life.

- **'Race'** is written in inverted commas to signify that the term is referring to social distinctions between groups rather than biological distinctions.

- **'Neighbourhood'** refers to the geographical area that fieldworkers are responsible for offering services in. This term is used because many fieldwork teams work within geographical boundaries. This is not to imply that neighbourhoods are synonymous with communities. By using this term, the author does not wish to negate any idea of communities of interest or imply that shared locality necessarily brings with it shared interests or relationships.

References

1 Department of Social Security (1990). *Households Below Average Income*. London, Government Statistical Service.

2 Becker, S. (1988). 'Poverty awareness' in Becker, S., MacPherson, S. (eds) *Public Issues, Private Pain*. London, Social Services Insight.

3 Popay, J., Dhooge, Y., Shipman C. (1986). *Unemployment and Health: What Role for Health and Social Services?* Research Report No. 3. London, Health Education Council.

GETTING STARTED

Introduction

The materials in this first section set the scene. Practice issues around poverty and health are sensitive issues that need to be explored in an environment where group members feel comfortable and able to participate. The materials provide an opportunity for your group to create an environment where current practice with families in poverty can be explored in a constructive way, and which will help the team to build up trust and confidence in each other. This section also encourages your team to check out your reasons for exploring poverty as an issue for practice and to think about how you will use the materials and deal with the issues that arise.

Aims of the Section

i) to clarify why poverty is an issue for the team;

ii) to encourage group identity;

iii) to develop confidence and trust between team members;

iv) to negotiate the nature, content and style of future meetings.

Team Activities

- 1A Hopes and fears game
- 1B Organising and negotiating check-list for future work

Information Sheet

- Thinking about the process

Notes for the Facilitator

- Ask team members to read the information sheet before coming to this session.

- This session sets the scene for the sessions that follow. Ensure that collaborative and participatory methods of learning and planning are central to this session. You may find it useful to read from some of the texts on group work methods identified in section 8 or consult with colleagues.

- The group may find this first session daunting, particularly if they have not participated in this kind of exercise before. Even though your team may be an established team, they may not be used to collective learning and planning. You will need to create a relaxed and non-threatening atmosphere: use an ice-breaker activity; make sure that you will not be disturbed; place the chairs in a circle; make arrangements for tea/coffee to be available.

- Think of some prompting questions that will help to stimulate and maintain the discussions.

- Ensure that you have read the introductory sub-section *Using this Handbook* and are generally familiar with the content and organisation of the materials in the handbook, particularly the team activity sheets.

- Be familiar with the timescale for using the team training handbook identified on page 5. Team members may ask questions about the time they need to commit.

Team Activity 1A

HOPES AND FEARS GAME

Estimated time: 1 hour
Method: brain-storm, group discussion
Materials: flip chart and pen

Relevant information sheet: *Thinking about the process*

This activity will help your team to clarify whether they wish to embark on a process of learning and planning in the area of family poverty and health. It will also help you to come to some agreement about whether these materials provide a useful way of making these central agenda items for the team.

1 **Brain-storm, as a group, to identify:**

   i) The things we would hope to get out of using these materials are .... (5 mins)
   e.g. *More information about the extent and nature of poverty ...*

   ii) The things that we fear about using the materials are ..... (5 mins)
   e.g. *It will take up too much time ...*

2 **Write the points you identify on a flip chart.**

3 **Use the points you identified in the brain-storm to discuss, as a group, the following issues:** (45 mins)

   i) How far does the team agree or disagree with the hopes that individuals identified?

   ii) Is everyone willing to accept changes in team strategies and methods?

   iii) What are our main concerns about using the materials to work on family poverty issues?

   iv) Which of these concerns can be allayed and which have no easy solution?

   v) What are our expectations for change, in terms of the work of individual team members and that of the whole team?

   vi) Are these expectations for change realistic?

Action Points!

*   Decide as a team whether you wish to continue to use these materials.
*   If so, move on to activity 1B.

Team Activity (1B)

ORGANISING AND NEGOTIATING CHECK-LIST FOR FUTURE WORK

Estimated time: 1 hour
Method: discussion, fill in check-list
Materials: copies of check-list

Relevant information sheet: *Thinking about the process*

Once your team has decided to continue to use these materials, it is important to spend some time thinking about how you will go about it. The following check-list will help you complete the organising and negotiating tasks identified in the information sheet. Work through each item in turn, ticking each task as the group discusses them and comes to some agreement about them. Add in any other areas you need to cover which may be specific to your group.

Check-List:

❏ Decide on the membership of the group.

Examine whether your group is able to incorporate a:
❏ Black perspective;   ❏ gender perspective;   ❏ disability perspective.

❏ Decide who else you might need to involve or consult at various stages.

❏ Decide when, where and for how long you will meet.

❏ Decide how you will run the sessions (for example, who will act as facilitator?)

❏ Read the section *Using the Team Training Handbook* (page 6).

❏ Check that everyone understands what group work methods of learning and planning involve.

❏ Consult or check out your decision to use these materials with your line manager if she/he is not participating in the sessions.

❏ Identify areas that are open to team decision-making and the limits of team autonomy.

❏ Negotiate a programme that will meet the needs of the group and the needs of your clients.

❏ Negotiate a set of ground rules for the group.

❏

❏

❏

Information Sheet

THINKING ABOUT THE PROCESS

It is important to spend some time thinking about how you will manage the process of reviewing fieldwork practice around poverty and health issues before you embark on the process itself. Managing the process involves three types of tasks: clarifying, organising and negotiating. Each of these tasks are discussed below.

Clarifying Tasks

The successful use of these materials depends on early clarification of a number of issues:

• **Does the team agree that poverty is an issue for their fieldwork practice?** Building an integrated and responsive service for families in poverty requires the commitment and co-operation of the whole team. Without this, the key stages of learning and planning identified in this handbook are unlikely to be completed successfully.

• **Are team members willing to make changes in their fieldwork practice?** Making poverty a central issue is likely to mean that your team will need to bring about significant changes to team objectives and fieldwork practice. You need to clarify and accept this at an early stage.

• **Are team expectations for change realistic?** Considerable obstacles stand in the way of radical change in fieldwork practice in the 1990s. For example, changes to local authority and health authority funding have altered the distribution of resources available for family work, while reforms emanating from the Children Act (1989) and the National Health Service and Community Care Act (1990) have redefined the roles of many health and welfare workers. These changing demands and obstacles, together with a recognition that the causes of poverty are structural rather than individual (see section 2), understandably may leave workers feeling powerless and unable to make an impact on poverty. While it is important to

realise that local health and welfare priorities and strategies are unlikely to challenge the structural causes of poverty, it is also important to recognise that local health and welfare work can have an important bearing on family health and well-being:

> • **it can ensure that family support strategies do not compound the effects of poverty on family life;**
>
> • **it can help families to mitigate or avoid the worst effects of poverty.**

• **Do team members feel happy to use participatory methods of learning and planning?** If people feel uncertain about the methods, they are unlikely to participate fully. Sharing fears and feelings within a group may help to allay people's concerns, and identify problems which may have no easy solution. If people remain unhappy or unprepared to make a commitment to use the materials, it may be more appropriate to find an alternative way of examining practice around poverty and health issues, or wait until there is a greater team consensus.

Organising Tasks

If your team considers poverty to be an important issue for them then this needs to be reflected in the arrangements you make to work through the materials. When organising and planning team sessions, you will need to consider the following issues:

• **Who should be involved?** Changes to the way services are delivered are unlikely to be successful unless all team members participate in the planning process. Workers such as health care assistants, nursery workers and administrative staff are team members yet they are often excluded from team planning sessions, even though they may be key deliverers of care. It is also important to consider whether the group is representative in terms of gender, 'race' and disability. If it is, then your work will be more likely to incorporate Black, gender and disability perspectives than if it is unrepresentative. You will need to consider whether you are able to incorporate these perspectives. If not, you will need help to do so, either by checking out the work you do from this handbook with a person/s who is able to advise on these perspectives, by arranging some team training on Black, gender or disability issues, or inviting other workers to join the team training.

• **When, where and for how long should the group meet?** Successful team work requires groups to make a commitment to meet on a regular basis for an agreed period of time. It may be necessary to obtain the permission and support of managers, and arrange for work commitments to be covered by colleagues.

• **How will the sessions be run?** Some groups will prefer to have one person to facilitate all the sessions, while others may prefer to rotate the facilitator's role at each session. The introductory section offers some guidance on the role of the facilitator.

• **Who needs to be consulted about a decision to work together on learning and planning around poverty?** Evaluating current practice with families in poverty brings with it the possibility that teams will need to change some aspects of their fieldwork practice. It is important that your team checks out with line managers that there is scope to set new goals and consider new ways of working. It is also useful to establish the limits of participatory management with the team leader early in the process: *what are the limits of team autonomy? Which areas of work are open to team decision-making?*

Negotiating Tasks

The process of negotiating underlines that the group has a shared responsibility for what happens in the group. It also creates an opportunity for the group to balance needs and expectations with the

objectives of the handbook. Below are some things that the group may find useful to negotiate:

• **Negotiate a programme that meets the needs of the team.** Your group may wish to spend longer working on some sections than others, or build in additional areas of work. For example, in section 3, which looks at what poverty means for family health and well-being, your team may identify that you need to arrange some anti-racism training before you move on to the next section.

• **Negotiate a set of ground rules for the team.** Negotiating a set of ground rules is a necessary activity in co-operative group work. It sets the boundaries for the group. Putting together a set of 'ground rules' enables groups to clarify the roles of both the facilitator and individual group members. It also helps to create an environment of trust and confidence. Below is an example of a set of rules that one group negotiated:

Our Group's Rules

1 Any input from a group member will be valued by the rest of the group.

2 Only one person will speak at any one time.

3 Anything said in the group will remain confidential to this group, unless the group gives permission for a matter to be discussed outside.

4 Every member of the group will take responsibility for keeping closely to the subject under discussion and for making sure that all members are encouraged to participate fully.

5 Everyone has equal status within the group, but the facilitator has the duty to keep the group to task!

! Team activity 1A will help your team to complete the clarifying tasks and team activity 1B will help you to complete the organising and negotiating tasks identified in this information sheet.

Summary and Conclusion

This section has offered a framework for your team to clarify whether poverty is an issue for them. It has emphasised the need for your team to confirm whether you wish to embark on a process of learning and planning and the need to spend some time organising the process. If you have completed the activities in this section you will be ready to move on to section 2!

Section 2 looks at how the term poverty is defined and explained. Poverty is not a neutral term. It means different things to different people and is shaped by our attitudes and beliefs about the nature of society and our knowledge of how families care. Section 2 examines these issues. It provides a framework for you:

• to examine the different meanings associated with the term poverty;

• to explore your attitudes to poverty and how these shape fieldwork practice.

DEFINING AND EXPLAINING POVERTY

Introduction

There is considerable controversy about which is the most acceptable way to define and explain poverty. When working with families, it is important to understand how views about poverty differ, and the consequences these views have for families and for health and welfare practice. The activity sheets in this section offer you an opportunity to explore your own attitudes and beliefs about poverty and to consider the consequences of your views for your fieldwork practice. The information sheets provide some background information on definitions and explanations of poverty.

Aims of the Section

i)   to explore how poverty is defined and explained;

ii) to examine personal and organisational attitudes to poverty;

iii) to examine how views about poverty affect fieldwork practice;

iv) to increase knowledge about the level and distribution of family poverty in the United Kingdom.

Team Activities

*   2A Definitions of poverty: taking a look
*   2B Clarifying views about poverty

Information Sheets

*   Defining poverty
*   Explaining poverty
*   Poverty in the United Kingdom

Notes for Facilitator

Activity 2A:

*   Encourage people to question whether each type of definition of poverty is wide enough rather than right or wrong;

Activity 2B:

*   Some team members may wish to challenge their colleagues' views about poverty. Ensure that any challenges are not personal;

*   Check out that your team definition of poverty is acceptable to the **whole** team. If you cannot reach a single agreed definition of poverty you will need to get the group to explore the reason for this. You can do this through discussion and by asking the team to widen their knowledge by reading some of the literature identified in section 8.

*   A working definition which accommodates a range of perspectives may need to be worked out. Agreeing to differ but finding some common ground is better than having no definition at all.

*   At the end of the session, ensure that team members are aware of which information sheets they need to read before the next session.

DEFINITIONS OF POVERTY: TAKING A LOOK

SECTION 2

Estimated time: 1 hour
Method: work in pairs, group discussion
Materials: copies of activity sheet, flip chart and pen

Relevant information sheet: *Defining poverty*

When working with disadvantaged families it is important to be clear about the views people hold about poverty – its definitions and explanations. This activity will help you to identify absolute and relative definitions of poverty and explore what the consequences of each type of definition may be for your practice.

1 **Below are some statements about poverty. Which statements do you consider reflect an absolute view of poverty, and which do you consider reflect a relative view of poverty? Begin by considering the statements in pairs** (5 mins)**, and then discuss them as a group.** (15 mins)

	Absolute	Relative
i) *Persons are beset by poverty when "resources are so small as to exclude them from the minimum acceptable way of life of the Member State in which they live."* [1]	☐	☐
ii) *"… A family is in poverty if it cannot afford to eat."* [2]	☐	☐
iii) *People "must have an income which enables them to participate in the life of the community."* [3]	☐	☐
iv) *"… the poor of today aren't there any more in a sense. They're a different sort of poor. Nobody's on the breadline. No one's standing in the gutter waiting for a crust to be thrown at them."* [4]	☐	☐
v) *People are in poverty when "they cannot have what the larger community regards as the minimum necessary for decency."* [5]	☐	☐

2 **As a group discuss the following points:** (40 mins)

• Which local situations/cases came to mind when you read the statements?

• Which statements do you find more acceptable than others, and why?

• What do you consider to be the *'minimum necessary for decency?'* (See statement e).

Team Activity 2B

CLARIFYING VIEWS ABOUT POVERTY

Estimated time: 2 hours
Method: working in pairs, group discussion
Materials: copies of the activity sheet, flip chart and pen

Relevant information sheets: *Defining poverty; Explaining poverty; Poverty in the United Kingdom.*

Our views about what creates poverty, together with our views about how we should define poverty, influence *what* services we offer to *which* families in poverty and *how* we offer them. This team activity is designed to help your team pin-point how you define and explain poverty.

1 **In pairs, discuss and answer the following two questions:** (15 mins)

   i) Which groups of families in the neighbourhood do we identify as 'in poverty' and why?

     e.g. *families with an unemployed head of household*

   ii) What do we consider causes poverty among the families we have identified as 'in poverty'?

2 **As a team, discuss what your answers tell you about the following issues:** (75 mins)

   i) Does the team work with particular groups of poor families and not others? If so, why?

     e.g. *Our agency's policy means that we can only offer services:*
       ... to people with a particular level of ill health or handicap;
       ... where a child has been or is at risk of being harmed.

   ii) At what level of financial hardship or distress does the team consider it appropriate to offer help?

   ii) What does the team's practice tell us about the team's definition of poverty?

   iii) How does the team explain poverty in the neighbourhood?

   iv) What has shaped the team's views? You should consider factors within the neighbourhood, organisational factors, and wider social and political factors, as well as personal experience.

   v) How does the way the team defines and explains poverty influence work:

     a) with individual families?

     e.g. *we do/do not talk to families about whether they can afford child safety equipment*

     b) the neighbourhood as whole?

     e.g. *we do/do not offer support to the tenants' housing action group.*

3 **As a team, write a definition of poverty that you consider to be an acceptable definition to underpin your work with families.** (30 mins)

Action Points!

- Write your team definition of poverty on a large piece of paper and pin it to the wall. Use it as a team statement about poverty in the planning exercises in the following sections.

- On a large piece of paper write up how your personal views and the views of your organisation influence:
  a) which families you work with;
  b) the level of financial hardship or distress at which you generally consider it appropriate to offer intervention;
  c) how your definition and explanation of poverty have, in the past, shaped your practice at individual, family and neighbourhood level.

Pin this paper to the wall and use it in future sessions to remind yourselves of how your views influence your daily practice.

DEFINING POVERTY

This information sheet examines different ways of defining poverty. Definitions of poverty fall into two broad categories: absolute definitions and relative definitions.

Absolute Poverty

Some people use an absolute definition of poverty. This definition, sometimes known as primary poverty, is closely associated with the work of the social reformer Seebohm Rowntree. According to the absolute view of poverty, a person is in poverty when his/her income falls below the minimum level needed for physical subsistence.

Families are in poverty when their incomes are "insufficient to obtain the minimum necessities for the maintenance of physical efficiency." [6]

Key features of this approach:

- It sees people as poor if they have an income below the minimum level of subsistence.
- It is based on the assumption that it is possible to identify a minimum level of subsistence.
- It is concerned with physical needs.
- It assumes that people's needs do not change over time.

The view that poverty is an absolute concept remains powerful in the United Kingdom (UK) today. An absolute definition of poverty is thought, by many social scientists, to form the basis of the social security system in the UK. While governments in the UK have not identified an official poverty line, the minimum income provided by income support is often taken as a surrogate/unofficial absolute poverty line. It certainly appears to represent the government's view of what is a minimum income for survival. This definition

still has many supporters, although few in academic circles.

What the critics say:

- It is very difficult to identify accurately an objective minimum standard of subsistence.
- A minimum standard of subsistence is not enough: people need the resources to stay healthy and participate in society.
- People's needs change over time according to what is socially acceptable. What was acceptable in the 1890s is not acceptable in the 1990s.
- People are social as well as physical beings: a definition of poverty is needed that takes account of this.
- Absolute definitions allow people to argue that there is no real poverty in Britain today, even though some people are poor in comparison to others: if poverty in the old absolute sense of hunger and want has been wiped out, then poverty no longer exists.

Definitions of absolute poverty still have applicability in parts of the industrially developing world, where famine remains an overriding concern. However, many people now think that absolute definitions of poverty are of little use in the Western world in the 1990s.

Relative Poverty

A relative definition of poverty offers an alternative to absolute definitions. This type of definition has been particularly associated with the research of Peter Townsend.[7] Relative definitions of poverty rest on the idea that poverty is relative to the kind of society we live in at a particular time. People are in relative poverty when their standard of living is poor in comparison to the standard of living of others.

> *"Individuals, families, and groups can be said to be in poverty when they lack the resources to obtain the types of diet, participate in the activities and have the living conditions and amenities which are customary, or at least widely encouraged or approved, in the societies to which they belong."* [8]

Key features of this approach:

- It sees people as poor if their standard of living is low relative to the rest of society.
- It is concerned with people's social and physical needs.
- It acknowledges that people's needs arise through their social roles and relationships – as parents, friends, partners, active citizens, or supportive neighbours – as well as through their need for physical survival.
- It sees poverty as about more than lack of money and poor living conditions: it is also about social exclusion and powerlessness.

While relative definitions of poverty take a wider view of people's needs than absolute definitions, they are not without limitations.

What the critics say:

- It can be difficult to identify what standard of living is the norm at any moment in time.
- Decisions about standards of living are not neutral: they are judgements about what is socially acceptable at a particular time.
- If poverty is relative it cannot be eradicated – there will always be groups who are poorer than others. Relative definitions confuse poverty with inequality.

The idea that poverty is relative to today's standards, and about more than physical needs, appears to be a view that is widespread. A MORI poll conducted for London Weekend Television found that large numbers of the population in Britain make decisions about what constitutes a minimum standard of living on social criteria (for example, having enough money to buy birthday presents), and not just on criteria for physical survival. This survey also highlighted that there is a public consensus that necessities for living are judged on today's standards and not on those of the past. [9]

How Do Definitions of Poverty Influence Fieldwork Practice?

The definition of poverty we hold has an important influence on policy and practice. It influences:

- who is defined as 'in poverty' and therefore, who is included in and excluded from the poverty statistics;
- whether poverty is considered to be a social issue that warrants intervention;
- the level of resources, locally and nationally, that are allocated to reduce poverty and assist poor families;
- which groups receive financial and material help.

! The way we define poverty is one of a complex of factors that shape our fieldwork practice with families. Team activity sheets 2A and 2B provide an opportunity for you and your team to think about how you and other people define poverty. Activity 2B also encourages you to work out a definition of poverty for your team. This definition will provide a starting point from which you will be able to move on, in the sections that follow, to plan responsive and flexible strategies for families in your neighbourhood.

EXPLAINING POVERTY

A key question for health and welfare workers, politicians, and policy makers alike is *'what creates poverty in a relatively prosperous industrial society?'* How we answer this question depends, in part, on our beliefs about the nature of poverty. Explanations of poverty fall into two broad groups: individual explanations and structural explanations.

Individual Explanations

Here poverty is seen as the consequence of personal inadequacy:

"If the poor didn't waste their money on cigarettes and new clothes...."

"People don't need more money, they just need to change their attitude!"

"There is nothing wrong with social security benefit levels. If more people knew how to budget properly, cook cheap meals and make do, there wouldn't be any poverty."

According to this type of explanation, poverty is the outcome of:

• failure to cope with daily living conditions;

• undesirable attitudes to budgeting, health and family relationships;

• irresponsible behaviour, particularly budgeting;

• skill and knowledge deficits.

This type of explanation is often associated with 'culture of poverty' theories.[10] Here, poverty is seen to be perpetuated when children internalise values, behaviours and spending patterns acquired from the family which they then carry into adulthood. Processes within the family are held responsible for the perpetuation of poverty, even if they are maintained by external forces.

Structural Explanations

According to this type of explanation, poverty is caused by social and economic factors that reduce the access of some social groups to income and essential material resources.

"If more people had jobs and decent wages there would be less poverty."

"People are poor because they do not have enough money to buy essentials."

Structural explanations suggest that the way society is organised and the shape of social and economic policies influence the conditions under which people live and work. Structural explanations suggest that poverty is the result of:

• poor access to employment and lack of childcare facilities;

• low wages;

• inadequate social security benefits;

• taxation policies that work disproportionately against the least well-off;

• the additional costs of caring.

Who is to Blame?

Research has continued to suggest that poverty is caused by structural factors rather than individual factors. It provides little evidence that the blame for poverty can be pinned on poor people themselves. To draw such conclusions does not, however, mean that individuals invariably make the most sensible and rational choices! But where does the responsibility lie for the structural causes of poverty? Most commonly, government policies are blamed for the creation and maintenance of structural inequalities and poverty in our society.

If we look back to the five main causes of poverty identified by structural explanations, we can see that the actions of governments, through social policies and legislation, can work to increase or alternatively reduce poverty levels in the UK.

But to pin the blame solely on governments is too simplistic. Golding[11] draws our attention to the way we, as members of society, are responsible for maintaining poverty and inequality:

'... poverty is created by the way society treats its least well-favoured members. It is inescapably wedded to the degree and consequences of social inequality we are prepared to tolerate or even encourage.'

This means we all have a responsibility to work for the reduction of poverty.

Regardless of where people put the blame for poverty, distinctions are often made between the 'deserving' and 'undeserving' poor. Some groups may be seen as less to blame for their poverty than others and therefore, more deserving of help. These distinctions may be based on age, gender, 'race', class or lifestyle. For example, children may be seen as more deserving than adults, and people with disabilities more deserving than people without disabilities. Those under retirement age but not in paid work (lone mothers and unemployed people) are most likely to be seen as undeserving, as are those who are perceived as having different characteristics, lifestyles or moral standards to the majority of people.

Even though we may explain poverty in structural terms, it does not mean that our attitudes are always consistent or unbiased.[12]

What Can Structural Explanations of Poverty Tell Us?

Structural explanations highlight that certain social groups bear the brunt of poverty.

• **They draw attention to the way social class, family structure, gender and 'race' appear to shape people's access to social and economic resources.** The causes of poverty are different for men and women, between ethnic groups, and between one- and two-parent families.

Social class:

• Families in social classes IV and V have heads of households who are in lower paid and less secure jobs than those in social classes I and II.

Family structure:

• The average weekly income for lone-parent families is considerably lower than that of two-parent families with the same number of children, yet the major

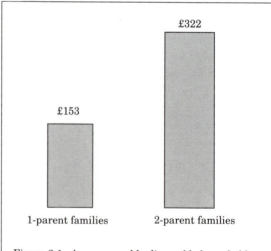

Figure 2.1: Average weekly disposable household income for one- and two-parent households with 2 or more children.

Source: Central Statistical Office (1990). *Family Expenditure Survey, 1989.* London, HMSO.

expenses of housing, food and costs relating to children remain the same.

'Race':

- Discrimination in education and employment means that Black and minority groups have a greater than average likelihood of being unemployed or in low paid jobs. [13]

- The experience of racism – in housing, education, health care, employment and leisure – further compounds the experience of poverty for Black and minority ethnic families.

Gender:

- Women tend to be concentrated in less well-paid and less secure sectors of the employment market than men.

- Women may be victims of hidden poverty: some women can be poor even in high-income families if they receive an inadequate share of the household resources.

- For Black and minority ethnic women, the experience of poverty and racism may be further compounded by sexism. In the domestic, social and employment spheres they often experience inequalities that stem from personal and institutional racism, as well as the gender inequalities of white women.

- **They draw attention to the way some groups incur extra daily living costs over and above those of other groups.** Family responsibilities, lone parenthood, old age, and sickness and disability create extra needs, and therefore extra costs, including the costs of additional heating, safe and appropriate housing, suitable and easily accessible forms of transport, and enough money for food and clothing. Those social groups that have to meet extra costs and have poor access to social and material resources are likely to experience the most extreme forms of poverty.

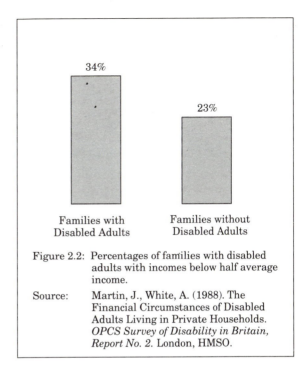

Figure 2.2: Percentages of families with disabled adults with incomes below half average income.

Source: Martin, J., White, A. (1988). The Financial Circumstances of Disabled Adults Living in Private Households. *OPCS Survey of Disability in Britain, Report No. 2.* London, HMSO.

How Do Explanations of Poverty Affect Practice?

Each type of explanation has its own consequences for fieldwork practice. Some of these consequences are listed below.

Individual Explanations:

- often encourage people to make distinctions between different groups of poor families, based on the idea of the 'deserving' and 'undeserving' poor;

- can lead to the view that clients do not necessarily have a right to welfare;

- can lead to practice responses that are often directed at individuals: interventions aimed to reduce personal inadequacies, change undesirable behaviour, etc., thus are often associated with victim-blaming;

- lead to practice responses that are often reactive rather than pro-active.

Structural Explanations:

- are likely to lead to the view that all people suffering deprivation and poverty need help;
- result in clients being likely to be seen as having a right to welfare;
- lead to practice responses that are likely to focus on the social and economic causes of poverty, and be concerned with health and social policies. Thus, they are less likely to be associated with victim-blaming;
- encourage practice responses that are pro-active rather than reactive.

Studies of health and welfare workers' beliefs about the causes of poverty highlight that, as a group, health and welfare workers are likely to offer a structural explanation of poverty.[14,15] However, the same research also shows that workers do not always translate the explanations they articulate into practice. In work with individuals, attitudes are not always positive, consistent or supportive towards poor families.

There is evidence to suggest that many workers find it easier to redefine financial and material problems as issues of personal or emotional inadequacy rather than find ways of working which take account of structural explanations. [16]

❗ Team activity 2B provides you with an opportunity to examine how group members define and explain poverty, and the way your views influence your practice. This activity sheet also encourages you to examine how political, social and organisational factors shape fieldwork practice.

POVERTY IN THE UNITED KINGDOM

This information sheet looks at the level and distribution of family poverty in the United Kingdom (UK). Before we examine poverty statistics it is important therefore to understand what they are actually measuring and how they measure it.

To measure poverty levels and map the distribution of poverty it is necessary to draw a line – *a poverty line* – between those who are poor and their better-off counterparts. Where the line is drawn depends on how poverty is defined and what is seen as a minimum level of income for family health and welfare. Poverty levels are usually measured in terms of household income, because income is thought to be a good measure of overall living standards within a household.

Poverty Measures in the UK

Unlike many other countries, the UK does not have an official poverty line. However, two unofficial poverty lines are commonly used to measure both the level of poverty in the UK and to identify those with poverty-level incomes.

1 Poverty line based on supplementary benefit/income support: (the most recent statistics relate to the period when supplementary benefit was in existence. Future statistics will be based on income support data).

This is the most extensively used poverty line in the UK and is derived from supplementary benefit/income support statistics. [17, 18] According to this poverty line:

- *anyone with an income on or below the level of supplementary benefit (100 per cent of benefit level) is '**in poverty**';*

- *anyone with an income between 100–140 per cent of supplementary benefit level is living '**on the margins of poverty**'.*

2 Poverty line based on average income: This is a relatively new poverty line. It can be calculated from the 'Households Below Average Income' statistics. [19] Using this poverty line:

- *anyone with an income on or below 50 per cent of average income is living '**in poverty**';*

- *anyone with an income between 50–60 per cent of average income is living '**on the margins of poverty**'.*

The way poverty is measured is frequently the subject of political debate. Poverty statistics tend to be used by anti-poverty groups and political parties in opposition to measure the performance of a government. If you wish to find out more about how poverty is measured and the advantages and disadvantages of each poverty line, you will find some references in section 8.

What Do Both Poverty Lines Have in Common?

- it can be argued that both poverty lines are very low, and thus they underestimate poverty levels;

- they both fail to give us any information on the distribution of poverty between different ethnic groups, or men and women;

- they only measure income at the level of the family or household: they fail to tell us about the distribution of poverty and income between different family members;

- they fail to include homeless people, or people living in prisons;

- they do not tell us **how long** people have been living in or on the margins of poverty: the problems associated with long-term poverty are different from, and often more severe than, those of short-term poverty.

Poverty Levels in the UK

As there is no one simple way to measure poverty this section will use both of the poverty lines identified above to show current national poverty levels and the distribution of poverty between social groups.

> **The figures indicate that, regardless of which poverty line is used, there has been a substantial rise in the number of people in poverty between 1979 and 1987 (latest available statistics).**

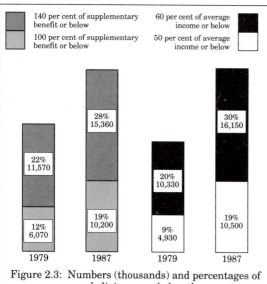

Figure 2.3: Numbers (thousands) and percentages of people living on or below the poverty line in the UK, 1979 and 1987.

Sources: Johnson, P., Webb, S. (1990). *Poverty in Official Statistics*. Institute for Fiscal Studies Commentary No. 24. London, Institute for Fiscal Studies. Department of Social Security (1990). *Households Below Average Income*. London, Government Statistical Service. Department of Health and Social Security (1989). *Low Income Families*. London, Government Statistical Service.

The statistics in figure 2.3 indicate different levels of poverty because they are measuring different things:

- figures based on **the level of supplementary benefit** (now income support) tell us that there has been an increase in the number of people with household income levels that fall below the minimum level set by government;
- figures based on **50 per cent of average income** tell us that there has been an increase in the number of people with incomes that fall below the average income.

Which Groups Are Poor?

Poverty is not evenly distributed between groups. The way society is organised and the impact of social policies renders some groups of people more vulnerable to poverty than others.

Official statistics tell us that those groups most at risk of poverty are:

- unemployed and low-paid people, particularly families with dependent children;
- people who are sick or have disabilities;
- older adults with pensions;
- lone-parent families.

Figure 2.4 shows the distribution of poverty (incomes below 50 per cent of average income) by family type in 1987.

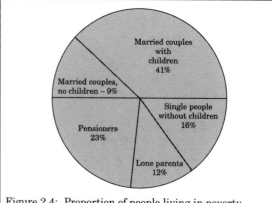

Figure 2.4: Proportion of people living in poverty (using 50 per cent of average income as the poverty line) by family type, 1987.

Source: Department of Social Security (1990). Households Below Average Income. London, Government Statistical Service.

Official statistics on household and family income do not tell us which ethnic groups or which individual family members are most at risk of poverty. However, other research studies tell us that Black and minority ethnic families are more at risk of poverty than white families and women are more at risk of poverty than their male partners.[20] These aspects of poverty will be discussed in section 3.

> **Families with young children now form the largest single group in poverty.**

Although the number of older adults in poverty remains high, since 1979 the burden of poverty has shifted away from older adults on to families with children. This rise in poverty among families with children means that a substantial and growing number of children are spending their formative years living in poverty. Figure 2.5 indicates that a quarter of all children in the UK now live in poverty:

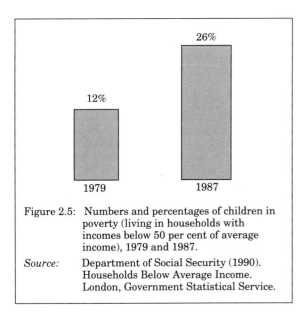

Figure 2.5: Numbers and percentages of children in poverty (living in households with incomes below 50 per cent of average income), 1979 and 1987.

Source: Department of Social Security (1990). Households Below Average Income. London, Government Statistical Service.

National poverty figures indicate that the number of families in poverty has increased significantly since 1979 and there is no indication that the 1990s will see a significant decline in the number of families bringing up children on low incomes and in adverse living conditions. This growth in family poverty has underlined the need for health and welfare workers to understand, and respond more effectively to, the needs of families in poverty. While national poverty levels draw attention to the fact that particular groups of families are especially vulnerable to poverty, they do not give any information about local poverty levels. Section 4 will provide your team with some guidelines to enable you to make an assessment of local levels and distribution of poverty.

Summary and Conclusion

This section has examined some of the ways in which poverty is defined and explained and has highlighted how views about poverty influence fieldwork practice and relationships with families. The activities in this section have provided you with the opportunity to check out how you define and explain poverty and to think about how your definitions and explanations shape your practice with families. If you wish to spend some more time looking at definitions and explanations of poverty, you will find some useful references in section 8.

References and Notes

1 Council of Ministers, EEC (1981). *Final Report of the First Programme of Pilot Schemes and Studies to Combat Poverty.* Brussels, Commission of the European Communities.

2 Joseph, K., Sumption, J. (1979). *Equality.* London, John Murray.

3 Chalker, L. (1979) House of Commons, 6th November, 1979.

4 Quoted in *New Society* 18/4/86.

5 Galbraith, J. (1970). *The Affluent Society.* Hamish Hamilton Ltd.

6 Rowntree, B. S. (1941). *Poverty and Progress.* London, Longmans, Green and Co. Ltd.

7 Townsend, P. (1979). *Poverty in the United Kingdom.* Harmondsworth, Penguin.

8 Townsend, P. (1979). ibid.

9 Mack, J., Lansley, S. (1985). *Poor Britain.* London, Allen and Unwin.

10 Brown, M., Madge, N. (1982). *Despite the Welfare State.* London, Heinemann.

11 Golding, P. (1986). 'Introduction' in Golding, P. (ed.) *Excluding the Poor.* London, Child Poverty Action Group.

12 Becker, S. (1988). 'Poverty awareness' in Becker, S., MacPherson, S. (eds) *Public Issues, Private Pain.* London, Social Services Insight.

13 Taylor, D. (1987). 'Living with unemployment' in Walker, A., Walker, C. (eds) *The Growing Divide – A Social Audit 1979 – 1987.* London, Child Poverty Action Group.

14 Becker, S. (1988). op. cit.

15 Popay, J., Dhooge, Y., Shipman, C. (1986). *Unemployment and Health: What Role for Health and Social Services?* London, Health Education Council.

16 Jordan, B. (1988). 'Poverty, social work and the state' in Becker, S., MacPherson, S. (eds) *Public Issues, Private Pain.* London, Social Services Insight.

17 Until 1988 this poverty line could be calculated from the Low Income Family Statistics which were published by the Department of Health and Social Security. These statistics have been discontinued. However, this poverty line can now be calculated from a new, but broadly similar, set of statistics published by the Institute for Fiscal Studies (see next reference).

18 Johnson, P., Webb, S. (1990). *Poverty in Official Statistics: Two Reports.* London, Institute for Fiscal Studies.

19 Department of Social Security (1990). *Households Below Average Income.* London, Government Statistical Service.

20 Millar, J., Glendinning, C. (1987). 'Invisible women, invisible poverty' in Glendinning, C., Millar, J. (eds) *Women and Poverty in Britain.* Brighton, Wheatsheaf Books.

POVERTY AS AN EXPERIENCE: DEVELOPING AN UNDERSTANDING

Introduction

Section 2 explored how views about poverty shape our perceptions of poverty and poor families and, therefore, how we work with families and what resources we provide for them. Exploring definitions and explanations only gives us a partial understanding of poverty. Poverty is a lived experience that families have to deal with on a daily basis. To understand poverty, we also need to develop an insight into what poverty means for families.

This section focuses on poverty as an experience for families and the complex interconnections between poverty, lifestyles and family health. The team activities encourage you to think about and question how you explain the link between the poverty that families experience and the health and well-being of the families you work with. The information sheets in this section provide some background information on the multidimensional nature of poverty and links between poverty and health.

Aims of the Section

i)   to raise awareness of the multidimensional experience of poverty;

ii) to increase knowledge levels about the links between poverty, health and well-being;

iii) to provide an opportunity for workers to examine how local families experience poverty;

iv) to identify the key elements of responsive service provision from the perspective of families.

Team Activities

- 3A Explaining the link between poverty and health
- 3B Poverty and family health in the neighbourhood

Information Sheets

- Experiencing poverty
- Poverty, health and well-being
- Why is income a key influence on health?

Notes for Facilitator

Activity 3A:

- Some team members may wish to challenge the views of their colleagues. Remind people at the beginning of, and during, the session that any challenges should not be personal.

- If you have difficulty coming up with an agreed statement on the link between poverty and ill health, try to identify why. If there are a wide range of views, encourage the group to find some common ground. It is better to have a statement that accommodates a range of views than no statement at all.

Activity 3B:

- Encourage team members to think about the interconnections between poor living conditions and choices that families make about health and childcare.

- Team members may sometimes revert to thinking about health and childcare choices in terms of individual pathology – it is important to get them to think about the way social and economic conditions shape choices. Suggest that team members ask some of the families they come into contact with over the next week how they think their material circumstances (their housing location, type of housing, etc.) and low income (money available for food and clothing etc) shape the way they care.

EXPLAINING THE LINK BETWEEN POVERTY AND HEALTH

Estimated time: 90 mins
Method: individual and group work
Materials: copies of this activity sheet, flip chart and pens

Relevant information sheet: *Poverty, health and well-being*

This activity provides an opportunity for you to look at how you explain the link between poverty and poor health. Some of the statements are deliberately contentious to help you to think through the issues.

1 **Below are some statements about poverty and health. In pairs, work through and discuss each statement. On your own sheet (you should have one each), tick whether you agree or disagree with each statement. You do not have to agree with your partner.** (15 mins)

	Agree	Partly Agree	Disagree	Not Sure
i) *Poor people usually don't care about their health. They would rather spend their money on booze and cigarettes.*	☐	☐	☐	☐
ii) *Families in poverty just don't have the living conditions or money for good health... They can't afford to make the sort of healthy choices that you and I can.*	☐	☐	☐	☐
iii) *In poor families, ill health is passed on through the generations. If parents are not healthy, then neither are their children. How can children grow up to be healthy if they learn the same unhealthy habits and reckless ways of their parents?*	☐	☐	☐	☐
iv) *Poor health makes people poor. If you're sick or disabled you can't work or get on in life like healthy people do.*	☐	☐	☐	☐
v) *If you are in poverty, you don't get the same opportunities that other people do. So people end up on the dole or in low-paid jobs. No wonder poor people have poorer health than better-off people.*	☐	☐	☐	☐
vi) *Poor people say they can't afford healthy food. I think they just need to make more economies... put on an extra jumper instead of turning up the heating and buy more fruit and vegetables instead of spending money on cigarettes.*	☐	☐	☐	☐

2   **As a group, work through the statements and discuss which statements you agree and disagree on:** (30 mins)

- is there any general consensus in the group? Are some statements generally more acceptable/unacceptable than others? If so, why?
- did you find any of the statements contentious? If so, why?

3   **As a group, try to identify which type of explanation of poverty and ill health each statement represents:** (use information sheet *Poverty, health and well-being* to help you). (15 mins)

- an hereditary/genetic explanation
- a health selection explanation
- a poor knowledge and attitudes explanation
- a poor budgeting explanation
- a lack of financial resources/structural explanation

4   **As a group, try to write a statement which represents the group's view about the link between poverty and ill health. If you can come up with an agreed statement:** (30 mins)

- write it on a flip chart and pin it to the wall;
- try to identify what implications the statement has for your work with families;

e.g.   *It means that we should think carefully about whether we should ask families to make more economies.*

We should think about changing the way we offer healthy eating advice.

POVERTY AND FAMILY HEALTH IN THE NEIGHBOURHOOD

Estimated time: 90 mins
Method: working in pairs, group discussion
Materials: flip chart, pens, copies of activity sheet and Poverty and Family Health
        Chart (page 34)

Relevant information sheets: *Experiencing poverty; Poverty, health and well-being; Income and health: the links*

This activity will help you to think through how poverty impacts on the health and well-being of the families that you work with. Use the Poverty and Family Health Chart (page 34) to help you to complete this activity.

1 **In pairs, think about two families in poverty that you work with** (you should each think about two different families).

  i)   Try to identify the structural causes of poverty in these families. Write them in Box A of the chart on page 34.

  ii) Identify all the aspects of their daily life that are affected by poverty and how (e.g. social life – cannot afford to go out with friends). Write this in Box B of the chart.

  iii) Identify how this experience of poverty affects the physical and mental health and behavioural choices (e.g. smoking, drug use, food choices) of the families you are thinking about. Write this in Boxes C, D, and E of the chart. (15 mins)

2 **Now place all your charts on a central table, or pin them up on the wall, so that everyone can see them.**

3 **Below are some questions for you to try to answer, as a group, about the information on your charts.** (75 mins)

  i)   What common health patterns can you identify from the information you have pooled about the families you have chosen to think about?

  ii) How does the research data on the link between poverty and health help you to explain these patterns?

  iii) Are some family members more affected by poverty and poor health than other family members? If so, who?

  iv) How does the research data help you to explain these differences between family members?

Action Points!

- In your regular team meetings, examine your team statement on the link between poverty and poor health and check out whether this statement is reflected in your team and individual practice.
- Keep your charts of how poverty affects the lives of some of the families in your neighbourhood. Pin them up on the wall to remind you of the links. You will find your diagram/s useful in the next section when you are deciding which information you need to collect for your poverty profile.

POVERTY AND FAMILY HEALTH CHART
(use with activity 3B)

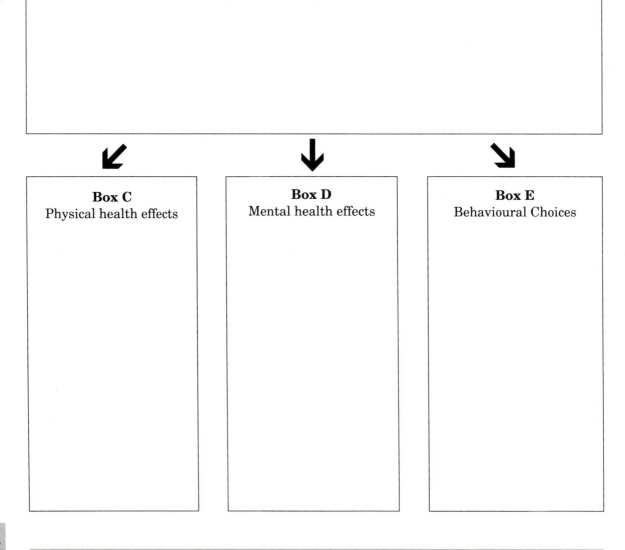

Box A
Causes of poverty

Box B
Aspects of daily living affected by poverty

Box C
Physical health effects

Box D
Mental health effects

Box E
Behavioural Choices

EXPERIENCING POVERTY

While poverty statistics alert us to the extent and distribution of poverty among families in the UK, they do not give any indication of what poverty means for families. Poverty needs to be examined from two angles. First, we need to look at the subjective experience of poverty: what families themselves say about the personal experience of poverty. Second, we need to take an objective look at the dimensions of poverty: what research data tell us about the daily living conditions and social circumstances of families in poverty.

What Do Families Say About Poverty?

I just wish we had a little more so our children could have what other children have.

(Mother of three children)[1]

[My son] sleeps on a mattress and so do I. The baby hasn't got a cot. We've only got two chairs, there's no carpets or proper curtains and we haven't got a three piece suite.

(Lone parent with two children)[2]

Our friends ask us out but we can't go because there's no money ... we're worse off than most people around here – you see everyone nicely dressed, and their kids nicely dressed, and we're in our old clothes.

(A couple with children)[3]

These quotes are from 'real' people – people talking about their everyday experiences of poverty. If a large number of first-hand accounts of poverty are examined, it is possible to pull out some common threads of experience.

Poverty is:

- an experience that permeates every part of family life;
- 'doing without' material goods and resources;
- a lack of opportunities for social relationships, fulfilment, and feelings of security;
- living in conditions that are unhealthy, unsafe and stressful;
- about making compromises in health, and social relationships.

While personal accounts alert us to the fact that families share some common experiences of poverty, they also remind us that the experience of poverty is not the same for all families.

- **The experience is different for men and women.** Women's accounts inform us that they bear the brunt of poverty. Women, through their position in the labour market, have a higher risk of poverty than men. Moreover, they appear to cushion the effect of poverty on their partners and children by cutting their own consumption and expenditure.

- **The experience differs for people from different ethnic groups**. For many Black and minority ethnic families, poverty is compounded by the experience of racism. Personal and institutional racism often mean that Black and minority ethnic people are in lower paid and less secure jobs, have less desirable housing conditions and receive poorer services than white people in poverty.

- **The experience is different for one-parent and two-parent families**. One-parent families tend to have lower incomes and less material resources for health and well-being than comparable two-parent families. Moreover, lone parents have to cope single handed with all the practical demands of budgeting and parenting, and with all the stresses of poverty.

• **The experience is different for people with disabilities and people without disabilities.** Disability brings with it a propensity towards poverty through poor employment opportunities, high dependency on inadequate benefits, lower wages, and greater living costs.

> **This diversity of experience highlights the fact that fieldwork strategies need to reflect the different needs and experiences of families in poverty.**

What Do Facts and Figures Say About Poverty?

Research on poverty informs us that poverty is a multidimensional experience for individuals and families:

• **Poverty is often associated with poor housing and for some families, homelessness:**

* Low income families often live in housing that is less suitable for caring for children, less spacious and less secure than higher income families (see figure 3.1).

* A significant number of families in poverty live in houses that are damp, overcrowded and poorly designed.[4]

* Families with heads born in the New Commonwealth or Pakistan are two and a half times more likely to live in unfit housing.[5]

* Homelessness is a growing problem among families in poverty. Approximately 356,000 households (686,000 people) were homeless in 1989.[6]

* One-parent families live in less secure housing conditions than two-parent families.[7]

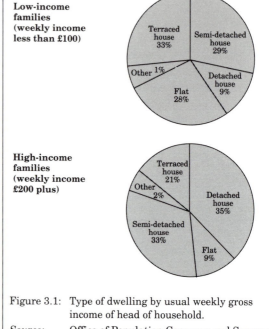

Figure 3.1: Type of dwelling by usual weekly gross income of head of household.

Source: Office of Population Censuses and Surveys (1989). *General Household Survey,* 1987. London, HMSO.

• **Poverty often means living in unhealthy and unsafe environments:**

* Families in poverty who live in urban areas are more likely to be housed in neighbourhoods that are unattractive, densely populated and have poorer health, social and educational facilities than other families.

* Families in poverty who live in rural areas are often isolated, live in insecure accommodation (tied cottages, summer lets and caravans) and may have to travel long distances for health and social facilities or to shop.

* Black families are more likely than white families to live in 'difficult to let' areas.

* Families in poverty are more likely to be exposed to environmental hazards such as air pollution, poor waste disposal, and heavy road traffic.

• Financial poverty means food poverty:

* Families in poverty may not have enough money to feed every member of the family, at each meal, each day. [8]

* Low-income families spend less in real terms on food but more as a proportion of weekly household expenditure than higher income families (see figure 3.2).

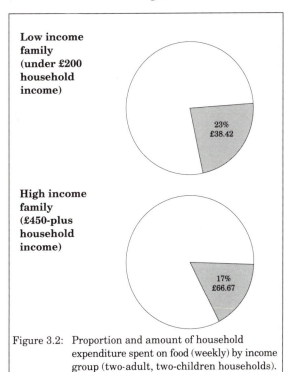

Low income family (under £200 household income)

23%
£38.42

High income family (£450-plus household income)

17%
£66.67

Figure 3.2: Proportion and amount of household expenditure spent on food (weekly) by income group (two-adult, two-children households).

Source: Department of Employment (1990). *Family Expenditure Survey, 1988.* London, HMSO.

* Poor families cannot afford the extra costs of buying healthy food. A healthy diet can cost up to 35 per cent more than an unhealthy diet.[9]

* Women bear the brunt of food poverty, often cutting back their own share of food to minimise the effects of poverty on other family members.

* The low availability and high costs of many traditional foods can increase the likelihood of food poverty for Black and minority ethnic families.

• Poverty often brings debt problems:

* A significant number of low-income families with children, particularly lone-parent families, have debts.[10]

* Housing and fuel costs account for a considerably larger proportion of the total weekly expenditure of low-income families than of higher-income families and are common causes of debt.[11]

• Poverty makes it difficult to care for children:

* The financial costs of caring for a child exceed the amount that parents receive from income support (see table 3.1).

Age of Child	Average weekly cost of caring	Income Support Rate	Income Support as proportion of cost of caring
0 – 4	£41.16	£12.35	30%
5 – 7	£48.02	£12.35	25%
8 – 10	£52.54	£12.35	23%
11 – 12	£57.14	£18.25	31%
13 – 15	£61.66	£18.25	29%

Table 3.1: Average weekly costs of caring (National Foster Care Association recommended allowances) compared with Income Support rates (1990).

Source: Oppenheim, C. (1990). *The Cost of a Child.* London, Child Poverty Action Group.

* Low income makes it difficult for parents to exercise the degree of control and choice that they would wish to make over childcare including diet, home safety, behaviour management, education and play.

I've got a real problem with Tom's sleeping. I can't get him to go down in his cot at night. She (the nursery worker) tells me to put him down and leave him. Well, that would be OK if we had more bedrooms, but Tom sleeps in the same room as the other two kids and he wakes them up with his crying. Their teacher is already saying that they need to go to bed earlier. People just don't realise how difficult it is for families like ours to put some of their ideas into practice!

(Mother with three young children, on income support)

* Parents in poverty appear to cope with some of the difficulties of caring in poverty by compromising one aspect of health for another and one person's health for that of another person:

I know that she doesn't get looked after as well as she should at Mrs ....'s, but she doesn't charge me much – it's all I can afford. If I want to feed and clothe her properly, I have to leave her while I go to work.

I would have liked to carry on breast feeding him but it's cheaper to bottle feed him and get free milk tokens. When I was breast feeding him I needed to eat a lot more to keep up my milk supply, and we couldn't afford it. Now I can manage on a sandwich and a cup of tea and use the money to make sure the others get enough food.

(Two mothers talking about making compromises)

Personal accounts and facts and figures highlight poverty as a multidimensional experience permeating every aspect of daily living. For families, poverty means not only struggling to make ends meet, but living in unhealthy conditions that cause worry, stress and feelings of powerlessness. If you wish to find out more about how poverty shapes childcare practices, you will find some useful references in section 8. The information sheet that follows looks at the links between poverty and poor health.

POVERTY, HEALTH AND WELL-BEING

The number of families living in poverty and unhealthy living conditions has increased significantly over the last decade. **But does poverty affect family health, and if so how?** This information sheet addresses these two key questions.

Does Poverty Affect Health?

The answer to this question is **yes!** No matter how you define health (in the narrow sense of absence of ill health or in a wider sense of physical, mental and social well-being[12]), there appears to be a strong relationship between poverty and poor health. At almost every age, people in poorer social groups have higher death rates and illness rates than people in wealthier groups:

* People in low-income groups have poorer physical health than people in higher income groups.[13]

* People in low-income groups have poorer mental health than people in higher income groups.[14]

* People in low-income groups suffer more stress than people in higher-income groups.[15]

* In 1986, babies born to parents in social classes IV and V were 1.5 times more likely to die in the perinatal period and 1.8 times more likely to die in the postneonatal period than babies born to social classes I and II parents.[16]

* Two-thirds of all low birthweight babies are born to working class mothers.[17]

* Children in social classes IV and V are twice as likely to die in childhood as their counterparts from social classes I and II.[18]

The evidence that low-income families have poorer health than better-off families is difficult to dispute. Although this evidence tells us that there is a link between poverty and health, it does not tell us what this link is.

How Does Poverty Affect Health?

People explain the link between poverty and poor health in different ways. The way we explain the relationship between poverty and health is often related to the way we explain poverty. Some of the commonly-used explanations are given below. The first four explanations can be described as individual explanations, that is, they explain the poor health of families in poverty in terms of individual characteristics. The fifth explanation can be described as a structural explanation, that is, it explains the poor health of families in poverty in terms of their poor access to material resources.

• **Hereditary factors?** This explanation suggests that people who are poor are unhealthy because they come from 'weaker' genetic stock. There appears to be no evidence to support this argument. Although there is a clear relationship between the health of parents and the health of their children, this can be explained in terms of the effect of environmental conditions rather than genetic disposition.

• **Health selection effect?** This explanation suggests that the poor health of low-income groups stems from the tendency of people with poor health to drift down the social scale, and therefore into poverty. There is evidence to suggest that people with long-term illness and disability have a higher risk of poverty than other groups. Although this relationship explains some of the association between poverty and poor health, it cannot entirely account for it.

• **Poor health knowledge or unhealthy attitudes?** This explanation is commonly used, especially to account for the poor health of Black and minority ethnic families. It appears to underlie much of health and welfare practice and many health education programmes and leads to interventions designed to increase health knowledge or change attitudes. However, a growing body of evidence suggests that the poor health of families in poverty does not stem from low levels of health knowledge and/or undesirable health attitudes. Research suggests that low-income families appear to have similar levels of health knowledge to other families and have similar health attitudes and orientations to other income groups.[19]

• **Poor budgeting and money management?** This explanation rests on the assumption that people are poor because of their own behaviour: they mismanage their money or spend it recklessly. It assumes that poverty-level incomes are adequate for families if only families would spend and budget wisely. Like the 'poor health knowledge and attitudes' explanation, this idea is clearly evident in health and welfare work. It forms the basis for interventions such as budgeting skills courses and budget cookery courses. There is little evidence to support this popular explanation. On the contrary, studies of budgeting patterns suggest that, within the limitations of low income, families manage their income and expenditure effectively. Indeed as a group, they allocate a greater proportion of their household expenditure to essential health resources, such as food, than higher income groups do.

• **Lack of financial and material resources for good health?** This explanation suggests that the poor health of families in poverty stems from their poor access to resources for health. Families in poverty tend to live in unhealthy living conditions and cannot afford to buy the resources that have been shown to be essential for good health: healthy food, adequate heating, transport, a safe environment, warm clothing, and social activities.

Much of the research supports the final explanation. It suggests that income rather than behaviour, attitudes or genetic disposition shapes the health of poor families.

What evidence is there to support a structural explanation?

There is evidence to suggest that there is a close relationship between income and health:

* Those groups with the highest income levels have the lowest death rates. As income levels fall, death rates rise.[20]

* The post-war widening of death rates between social classes is related to the trend in relative poverty. When relative poverty has increased, inequalities in health have widened. There is evidence that the widening in health inequalities in the 1970s and 1980s is related to increases in relative poverty levels. [21]

* Social class differences in health have been found to reflect differences in income levels.[22]

Evidence suggests that being healthy requires more than just enough income to stay alive. It requires a decent level of income relative to other people: an income which allows low-income families to benefit from similar living standards to better-off families.

The next information sheet looks at the relationship between income and health.

WHY IS INCOME A KEY INFLUENCE ON HEALTH?

Poverty appears to be a key determinant of health. This information sheet examines the relationship between income and health. Research on social inequalities in health has often tried to address the relationship between social position and health rather than the specific relationship between income and health. Although less is known about the relationship between income and health, the evidence that is available provides a valuable insight into the important role that income plays in family health.

> **Household income is the greatest determinant of family living standards. It touches every part of human life.**

Household income influences:

* where a family lives, therefore their degree of exposure to environmental hazards, access to space and social support structures and access to leisure, work, educational and health facilities;

* the quality of housing, and therefore a family's degree of exposure to diseases associated with cold and damp;

* how much money is available for food, fuel and clothing, thus the body's capacity to regenerate and resist disease.

Together these resources determine a family's degree of domestic comfort and contribute to their sense of physical, social and emotional well-being.

Poverty affects health in a complex way. It is possible to identify three main processes[23] by which poverty shapes family health and family health care. They are described below.

While these processes have been separated here to illustrate how they operate, in reality, they are interconnected rather than individual processes.

Processes By Which Poverty Affects Health

• **Physical processes:** The direct effect of poverty on physical health is probably the most well-researched and easily understood process. It fits in well with our understanding of the most commonly used model of disease causation, the medical model. Poverty directly affects health by restricting access to the basic necessities for good health, such as a nutritious diet, good housing, warmth and a safe environment. An example of this process is the way poor diet restricts growth and development, and increases susceptibility to disease.[24]

• **Psychological processes:** Living in poverty exposes individuals and families to high levels of stress. Money and high social status buy choice and the opportunity to solve problems. They also bring domestic comfort. Poverty allows little scope to cope with either the day in, day out stress of living below the bread-line, or the stresses of life events such as bereavement, loss of employment or relationship breakdown. The stresses of poverty have been shown to lead to poor physical and mental health, as well as shaping behavioural choices.

• **Behavioural processes:** The idea that health is shaped by behavioural processes is not new. However, traditional models usually rest on the assumption that choices about health behaviour lie within the control of the individual. Research from the social sciences has drawn attention to the limitations of this model. Behaviour does not occur in a vacuum: it is shaped by the social and economic circumstances of people's lives. Research[25] has illustrated how the health behaviour of families in poverty is constrained by low income. For example, some of the health problems of families in poverty are likely to result from the way low income constrains choices over food or childcare. Certain behaviours also act as coping strategies that help low-income families to deal with, and survive, the stresses and financial hardships of family life in poverty. For example, cigarette smoking can play a crucial role in the lives of mothers in poverty. It appears to help them to cope with the psychological stress and financial hardship of parenting in poverty. Many mothers say they continue to smoke because the benefits (ability to cope) outweigh the health risks or financial costs of smoking.[26]

Figure 3.3 indicates the nature of the relationship between health and poverty.

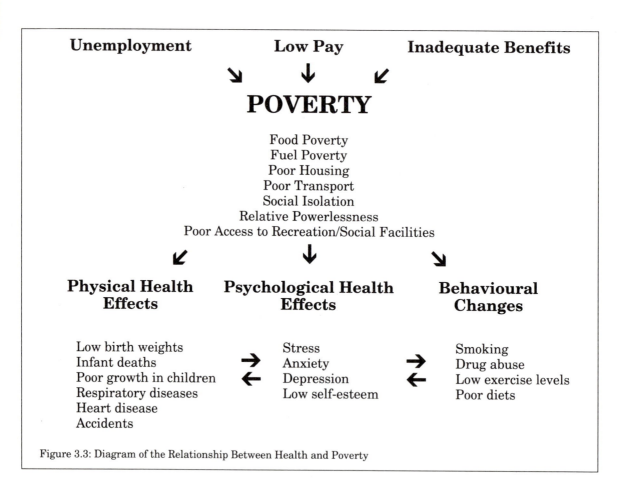

Figure 3.3: Diagram of the Relationship Between Health and Poverty

Summary and Conclusion

This section has provided an opportunity to consider how poverty may be affecting the local people you work with and how some of the health problems they experience can be explained. It has highlighted that poverty is a multidimensional experience that permeates the whole of family life and family health. The relationship between poverty and health cannot be explained in terms of the knowledge, attitudes, behaviour or genetic disposition of individuals or a health selection effect. The poor health of families in poverty appears to stem from their poor access to health resources.

The next section will enable you to begin to make an assessment of poverty levels and the impact of poverty on the neighbourhood in which you work.

References and Notes

1 Quoted in Oppenheim, C. (1990). *Poverty: The Facts.* London, Child Poverty Action Group.
2 Quoted in Oppenheim, C. (1990). ibid.
3 Quoted in Barnardos (1990). *Missing the Target.* London, Barnardos.
4 For a discussion on housing patterns see Blackburn, C. (1990). *Poverty and Health: Working with Families.* Chapter 4, 'Housing conditions and health'. Buckingham, Open University Press.
5 Department of the Environment (1986). *English House Condition Survey.* London, HMSO.
6 Greve, J., Currie, E. (1990). *Homelessness in Britain.* Joseph Rowntree Memorial Trust.
7 National Council for One Parent Families (1989). *70th Annual Report.* London, National Council for One Parent Families.
8 For more information and references on food poverty see Blackburn, C. (1991). op. cit. Chapter 3, 'Food and poverty'.
9 Cole-Hamilton, I. (1988). *Review of Food Patterns Amongst Low Income Groups in the UK.* A Report to the Health Education Authority (unpublished).
10 Berthoud, R. (1989). *Credit, Debt and Poverty.* Research Paper No. 1, Social Security Advisory Committee. London, HMSO.
11 Department of Employment (1989). *Employment Gazette,* May, 1989.
12 Health can be defined in a number of ways. Most people now agree that it is important to operate with a wider definition of health, where health is seen as physical, mental and social well-being. If you wish to do any further reading on definitions and concepts of health in relation to families, see Blackburn, C. (1991). op. cit. Chapter 6, 'Caring for children's health in poverty'.
13 Blaxter, M. (1990). *Health and Lifestyles.* London, Routledge.
14 Blaxter, M. (1990). ibid.
15 See Blackburn, C. (1990). op. cit., Chapter 5, 'Parents: stress, coping and health behaviour'.
16 Whitehead, M. (1987). *The Health Divide.* London, Health Education Council.
17 Whitehead, M. (1987). ibid.
18 Office of Population, Censuses and Surveys (1988). *Occupational Mortality: Childhood Supplement 1979–80, 1982–83.* London, HMSO.
19 See Blackburn, C. (1991). op. cit. Chapter 3, 'Food and poverty'.
20 Wilkinson, R. (1989). 'Class mortality differentials, income distribution and trends in poverty 1921–1981'. *Journal of Social Policy,* Vol. 18, No. 3: 307–35.
21 Wilkinson, R. (1989). ibid.
22 Blaxter, M. (1990). op. cit.
23 British Medical Association (1987). *Deprivation and Ill-Health.* London, British Medical Association.
24 British Medical Association (1987). ibid.
25 Graham, H. (1984). *Women, Health and the Family.* Brighton, Wheatsheaf Books.
26 Graham, H. (1984). ibid.

ASSESSING POVERTY AND POOR HEALTH

Introduction

This section looks at how your team can assess the impact of poverty on local families, and at the ways local health and welfare services are responding. The process of assessing poverty levels provides a valuable opportunity to re-appraise policies and practices.

Developing an information base is the first step in the process of planning services to meet the needs of families in poverty. You may feel that you already know about the level and extent of poverty and the health problems that exist in your area. However, you will still find this section useful to complete: it gives you an opportunity to check out whether the assumptions you are working with are accurate.

Aims of the Section

i)   to identify how workers can collect information for a poverty and health profile;

ii) to enable team members to think critically about information they have or need;

iii) to examine how information from poverty and health profiles can be analysed.

Team Activities

- 4A Collecting information
- 4B Analysing poverty and health profile information
- 4C Deciding what to do with poverty and health profile information

Information Sheets

- Poverty and health profiles: what are they, why use them?
- Building a poverty and health profile: guidelines for collecting information
- Thinking critically: guidelines for analysing information

Notes for Facilitator

- This section may take a long time to complete, especially if your team is compiling a poverty and health profile from scratch. Reassure people that it is OK to spend this amount of time on this section: it will have major advantages for work planning over a long period.

Activity 4A:

- Make sure the group sets itself a realistic timescale to complete any profiling tasks. You will need to allow enough time between activities 4A and 4B to allow you to set about collecting information.

- You will need to decide before this activity (at a team meeting) whether you are going to collect information with residents or as a team. If you are going to collect information with local people, you will need to check out that local people agree to using this activity. If not, you could adapt it to fit in with their wishes or devise an alternative activity.

- Following this activity, check periodically that everyone is clear about their tasks and is able to keep to the timescale. If necessary, re-negotiate the timescale or find out whether workloads can be redistributed.

Team Activity 4A
COLLECTING INFORMATION

Estimated time: 3 hours
Method: brain-storming and group discussion
Materials: flip chart and pen, copies of Collecting Information Matrix (page 48)

Relevant information sheets: *Poverty and health profiles: what are they, why use them? Building a poverty and health profile: guidelines for collecting information*

This activity will help you to collect information for your poverty and health profile. The matrix will help you to work out what information you need and what information you already have, which sources you need to gain access to and what types of information need to be collected. This activity can be used whether you are collecting information jointly with residents (if they find it acceptable) or as an agency team.

1 **What do we need to know?** (1.5 hours)
   i)   Begin by brain-storming, as a group, to identify all the types of information that could be useful to you.
   ii) Examine the list and cross off those items that are not essential.
   iii) Examine the items that are left and decide which of these items are unrealistic to collect within the limits of time and resources. Cross them off the list or consider other ways of collecting them (e.g. find out whether students could collect this information as part of an assignment).
   iv) Write down the items that remain in column 1 of the matrix.

2 **Which information do we already have?** (30 mins)
   i)   Pool your knowledge to identify which information you already have access to. Place a tick in column 2 of the matrix by any item that you already have.
   ii) Write down where it is located in column 3 of the matrix.

3 **Which information is available elsewhere?** (30 mins)
   i)   Identify which of the items in column 1 of the matrix are available from other sources, and place a tick by them in column 4.
   ii) In column 5 of the matrix write down where this information is available.

4 **Organising the collection procedure:** (30 mins)
   i)   Decide who will be responsible for collecting which information. Write this in column 6 of the matrix.
   ii) Decide whether workloads need to be altered to allow this work to take place. Note what action needs to occur.
   iii) Agree on a timescale. How long will you allocate to complete this task? Be realistic – it will take you weeks rather than days.
   iv) Decide on a date for a follow-up session to check progress.

SECTION 4

Action Point!

Ensure that before embarking on the next team activity you have a meeting to check how you are progressing with information collection.

COLLECTING INFORMATION MATRIX
(use with activity 4A)

1 Information needed	2 Information we have	3 Location of information	4 Information elsewhere	5 Location of other information	6 Person to collect

ANALYSING POVERTY AND HEALTH PROFILE INFORMATION

**Estimated time: 3–4 hours, depending on how much information you have collected.
You could split this session into two if necessary
Method: individual presentations, group discussion
Materials: information collected (you will need copies of statistical information etc.
You could use photocopies or use an overhead projector and acetates)**

Relevant information sheet: *Thinking critically: guidelines for analysing information*

This activity will help you to draw out some of the key information from the information you have collected. *Before you come to this session, you should each ensure that you are familiar with the information you have collected individually.* Be able to present the information briefly and say what you think it is telling you.

1   **Work through the main pieces of information. The person/s who collected it can briefly present it and say what s/he thinks are the key points that come out of the information. Of each piece of information, ask the following questions:** (90 mins – make sure you have a break!)

   i)   Is it reliable and accurate?

   ii)   Are there any additional points about it that the presenter has not noted?

   iii) Are there any alternative explanations to the one given? If so, which explanation appears to be the most accurate?

   iv)   Can we accept this information as relatively accurate or should we discard it or check it out further?

Ask your facilitator to keep a record of all the points you make, and agree and disagree on, on a flip chart. If there are areas of disagreement you will need to try to establish the reasons for this and try to resolve them. Some things that may help are time-tabling another session for more discussion, gathering further information or checking out analyses with other people (residents, other workers, information officers, academics, etc.)

2   **Once you have worked through the main pieces of information, try to answer some of the following questions:** (90 mins)

   i)   What are the common trends and patterns in the neighbourhood?

   ii)   What are the neighbourhood's strengths and resources?

   iii) What are the major unmet needs/problems in the neighbourhood?

   iv)   Are there any links between needs and problems (for example, are high child-accident levels linked to poor housing and overcrowding?)

   v)   Which health needs can families meet for themselves?

   vi)   Which issues/problems do families need help with from our team/agency?

   vii) Which issues/problems do families need help with from other agencies and organisations in the neighbourhood?

SECTION 4

viii) How effective are we at helping families to meet their needs using our current goals, strategies and methods of practice?

(You do not need to go on to identify goals, strategies and methods at this stage as an activity in the next section will help you to do this.)

Action Point!

You may like to spend 10 minutes going back to the work you did in activities 2A and 2B. See whether some of your perceptions about which families were poor were accurate, according to your poverty and health profile information. You may be surprised to find how much your knowledge and information base has grown!

DECIDING WHAT TO DO WITH A POVERTY AND HEALTH PROFILE

Estimated time: 1 hour
Method: group work
Materials: flip chart and pens

Relevant information sheet: *Thinking critically: guidelines for analysing information*

Your poverty and health profile will contain a rich seam of information that will be of use to other people, as well as helping your team to set goals and objectives for your own work. This activity will help you to decide how to write up and disseminate information from your poverty and health profile. Work through the questions below as a group, and try to decide which option/s to take. Place a tick by any option you choose. The options listed here are only suggestions. You may be able to think of options that are more appropriate for your team.

1 How will you write up your profile?
   *   put the information on to a word processor ☐
   *   put the information on individual sheets in a ring binder ☐
   *   have the information printed and bound into a report ☐
   *   have a full report for your use and a shorter, more accessible one
       for other people to look at ☐
   *   ☐
   *   ☐

2 How will you make the information useful and accessible to local people?
   *   hold local meetings ☐
   *   leave copies, or shorter versions, of the profile in reception areas,
       community centres, etc. ☐
   *   have a short report published in a local newssheet ☐
   *   offer copies to local groups ☐
   *   ☐
   *   ☐

3 Who else will you disseminate the findings to?
   *   your manager ☐
   *   colleagues in other teams ☐
   *   workers in other agencies and organisations ☐
   *   local councillors ☐
   *   ☐
   *   ☐

4   How will you disseminate your information to other workers?

* at workers' forums ☐
* at routine inter-agency meetings ☐
* put together a display ☐
* hold a special meeting ☐
* at trade union or professional body meetings ☐
* ☐
* ☐

Action Point!

Over the next few months, carry out any dissemination plans you have agreed. Make a date to discuss your dissemination progress at future team meetings.

POVERTY AND HEALTH PROFILES: WHAT ARE THEY, WHY USE THEM?

Making an assessment of local poverty levels and the impact of poverty on family health and well-being in the neighbourhood is a crucial step in the process of developing responsive services for families in poverty. A poverty and health profile is a key to making this assessment. This information sheet explains what poverty and health profiles are, and looks at the value of using them.

What is a Poverty and Health Profile?

The Oxford Dictionary defines the term 'profile' as an outline, or short biographical or character sketch. In the context of health and welfare work, a poverty and health profile can be described as an outline, or account, of poverty levels and poverty-associated problems in the neighbourhood.

The idea of profiling is not new. Health profiles, neighbourhood studies and community appraisals have been used by health and welfare workers as a way of looking at the needs of local communities and identifying gaps in services for some time. We have chosen to use the term 'poverty and health profile' not to indicate that poverty and health profiles are different from community appraisals or neighbourhood studies, but because the term spells out that it is a specific attempt to assess poverty levels and poverty-related problems. Workers who already use profiles or appraisals in their work may simply need to add a poverty component to, or modify, their existing profiles.

Why are Poverty and Health Profiles Useful?

Below are some reasons why poverty and health profiles are useful. They can allow teams to:

* check out whether assumptions about families and neighbourhoods are accurate;
* incorporate what local people identify as their needs and say about services into planning;
* monitor the impact of poor living conditions, low income and stress on local families;
* identify local needs, demands for services, and gaps in service provision;
* plan more responsive and effective services for families;
* monitor the impact of, and evaluate, local service provision;
* present a sound case to budget holders in bids for resources, using valid and comparable data.

A Note of Caution!

Although an information base is an invaluable tool, there is a tension between collecting and recording information to identify unmet needs and prying into the lives of residents. What or who gives local workers the mandate to gather information on residents? The answer is no one! Critics of community work models have expressed concern about how information is used by workers. They point out that information is not always used in the best interests of local people.[1] While there is no easy solution to these tensions, there are several steps that workers can take to ensure that ethical dilemmas are minimised:

• **Consider making information collection a joint activity between residents and workers.** Poverty and health profiles can be tools for local people to use for their own benefit and to argue for better health and social resources for their

SECTION 4

neighbourhood. There are several advantages to the joint collection of information:

* it harnesses the knowledge and skills of both local people and workers;
* it can lead to greater trust and co-operation between professional and lay people;
* it can lead to more appropriate service provision;
* it increases professional accountability.

We have been working with a neighbourhood profile for a couple of years. Adding more information on poverty has helped us to be clearer about why so many of the people we work with have health problems. It has focused our work. We have worked with the families who use the family centre to build up a picture of how poverty affects their lives.... The information has been useful to some of the groups who use the centre, as well as to us. One group used the information on local play facilities and accidents in their campaign to get more safe play areas on the estate.

(A community worker at a family centre)

• **If information collection is not a joint activity:**

* do not be secretive about it. Tell people what information you are collecting and why!
* consider how you can avoid information being used to 'label' groups or neighbourhoods by ensuring that you include information of neighbourhood strengths;
* ensure that local people jointly own or have easy access to collected information (with the exception of confidential client information). Put copies of profiles in the local library, waiting rooms, etc. If it is about their community, let local people see it and use the information to their advantage;
* only collect information that is essential and can be considered, by both workers and residents, to be in the best interests of the community.

Building Poverty and Health Profiles

There are three main stages to building a poverty and health profile:

Stage 1: Collecting information – deciding what information is needed, identifying where information can be found and who will collect it, collecting information and filling in the gaps.

Stage 2: Analysing information – thinking critically about collected information, deciding what it tells you and pulling out key points.

Stage 3: Using information – setting goals and planning services.

Guidelines for completing stages 1 and 2 are given in the information sheets that follow. Stage 3 of the poverty profiling process will be discussed in the next section.

BUILDING A POVERTY AND HEALTH PROFILE: GUIDELINES FOR COLLECTING INFORMATION

This information sheet provides a set of guidelines that will help you to identify which information you need to collect for a local poverty and health profile and to carry out the activity itself. Below are some key questions to ask about collecting information. These questions are relevant whether you intend to collect information with local people, other agencies or by yourselves.

What Do We Need to Know About Family Poverty and Service Provision in the Neighbourhood?

• **Decide which things are essential.** It is useful to remember the purpose of a poverty and health profile when collecting information: to assist planning and the development of services. Set yourselves a realistic target. Profiling is not a one-off exercise. You can collect essential information first and add other information when you have time and when new information becomes available.

• **Collect information that reflects the concerns of residents as well as workers.** This means collecting information that will allow you to see which issues residents identify as important and how they define them.

• **Decide which poverty-line you are going to use.** If you refer back to section 3 you will remember that there is more than one way of measuring the level and distribution of poverty. You will not be able to collect the kind of data that national poverty levels are based on, but you could identify as 'in poverty' those on income support, family credit or in receipt of housing benefit, or use a measure of your own.

Some of the main things you will want to find out about are:

* *The level of and distribution of poverty among local families:* How many families are poor? Which groups of families appear to be most at risk of poverty (for example, lone-parent families; families with people with disabilities)? Which individuals within families appear to be poorer than others? Are poor families concentrated in particular parts of the neighbourhood/types of housing stock?

* *The impact of poverty on the health and well-being of local families:* How do material and social conditions affect families directly, and indirectly by shaping their behaviour and choices about health, welfare and education? How does poverty appear to affect the social relationships of families, and social relationships within the neighbourhood as a whole? What is the health status of poor families in the neighbourhood? For example, how many babies are born with low birth weights? How common are stress and depression among parents in poor families?

* *What do families identify as their personal and material support needs?* For example, what do parents feel they need help with to keep their children safe in the home or to ease some of the tensions of bringing up children in adverse conditions?

* *The living conditions of local families:* What are the housing conditions, environmental conditions and transport facilities in the neighbourhood, and how do these affect parents' ability to care for children?

* *The level of and demand for services:* For example, what is the demand for and use of the welfare rights advice sessions at the community centre or the demand for childcare provision?

SECTION 4

55

* *The gaps in service provision, in your agency and other agencies:* For example, where are the gaps in provision for carers of people with disabilities or for African Caribbean families?

* *The strengths and positive aspects of the neighbourhood:* What factors in the neighbourhood act to support families and what factors increase their vulnerability? For example, do local social networks support or fail lone parents with young children?

* *Factors which create and maintain family poverty in the neighbourhood:* For example, how do local employment policies affect families? Do local authority charging policies increase the financial difficulties of low-income families?

It is not possible to be over-prescriptive about what you need to know. While the information identified above will be central to all poverty and health profiles, you may want or need to collect other information, but this will depend on time, and local needs and circumstances. At the end of this information sheet, you will find a list of the types and sources of information that will be of use.

Which Kinds of Information Will Tell Us What We Need to Know?

• **First identify the questions you need to answer, then collect relevant information.** If you collect information on an ad hoc basis and then try to identify key factors, you are likely to waste a lot of time and energy.

• **Remember, particular types of data will only answer particular questions.** For example, referral or caseload statistics will tell you how many and what type of individuals and families use your services but it cannot tell you what clients thought of your services. Quantitative information will help you to answer questions concerned with how many,

who, what, where and when, while qualitative information will help to answer 'why' and 'how' questions and find out what people think of services and identify as their needs.

Which Information Do We Already Have?

It is likely that some of the information you have identified is already available to your team, for example, information on service users and staff activity. Identifying what is readily available is a useful starting point. People are often surprised to find they hold valuable information in their own bases.

Which Information is Available from Another Department, Agency or Organisation?

• **Other departments in your agency, and other agencies and organisations will have information that is useful to you.** Some useful sources are identified at the end of the section.

• **You will have to negotiate access to information:**

* find out who is the main gatekeeper to information;

* explain clearly to gatekeepers why you would like access to the data;

* you could emphasise that your team is looking at ways of making the team more effective and efficient (these phrases go down well when resources are scarce!), more responsive to the needs of your clients, trying to respond to the local anti-poverty strategy (if one exists) or trying to meet its responsibilities under the Children Act (1989).

Your manager may be able to help, either by backing up your request, or by obtaining information on your behalf.

Which Information is Not Available but Would be Useful?

• **When you have found out what information is already available, you will be able to identify any gaps.** Filling in the gaps is likely to be the most difficult part of poverty profiling but it will provide the opportunity to review your recording procedure generally.

• **You will be able to fill in some of the gaps by collecting information yourselves.** If you decide to collect information yourselves:

* be systematic about how you collect information;

* collect information in a format that can be analysed.

Some easy ways to collect information

* *Record particular types of information on a computer if available, or easily identifiable and retrievable parts of existing records or on client index cards:* for example, you can record housing problems, welfare benefits information or whether lone- or two-parent family on client index cards or at the front of the records. You need to be able to identify general trends and common problems at a glance.

* *Use large scale maps of the neighbourhood and coloured pins* to record where particular types of referrals are coming from, where particular types of incidents/problems occur (for example, child accident rates and child abuse rates), or the distribution of neighbourhood facilities. Be careful not to pin-point individual houses though!

* *Hold meetings, local forums or visit local groups* to get consumer views or feedback on services.

• **In some instances, it may be more appropriate for someone else to collect this information for you.** The research and information department of your agency or a local polytechnic or university may be willing to collect the information for you (if the information can also be used for their own research). You may be able to argue, through your team or area manager, that particular kinds of information need to be collected on behalf of all teams on a routine basis to provide comparable information. While you may think that you have very little influence over which kinds of information need to be collected at area level, remember that information and research officers will not know what your information needs are if you do not make any effort, through line management, to tell them!

Some Useful Types and Sources of Information for Poverty and Health Profiles

Below is a list of some types of information/data that will be useful for your profile. This is not intended to be an exhaustive list as the type of information you will need will depend, to some extent, on local circumstances. Nor should you think that you need to collect all of this information – the list is there to give you some ideas.

Some main sources of information are:
* Local authority research and planning departments;

* Health authority information departments and Family Health Service Authorities;

* Local universities and polytechnics: their prospectuses and reports will identify likely Departments, Research Centres (look for ones with Health, Social Studies or Employment in the title!), and teaching or research staff may be helpful;

* Voluntary or watch-dog organisations: such as your local Community Health Council and Citizens' Advice Bureau.

- **Sources of different types of information:**

Type of information	Source
Direct data on poverty Numbers of families with incomes on or below the poverty line – claiming or entitled to income support/disability allowances/ housing benefit.	
i) in the neighbourhood	social security office, housing benefit office
ii) service users	referral/caseload analysis
Population data Age/sex breakdown	census, referral/caseload analysis
Social class composition	census data
Ethnic mix/languages/ religions	census (from 1991), ethnic monitoring systems
Availability of social support	information from local people and workers
Family status/structures, e.g. number and percentage of lone-parent families, extended families	census data, referral/caseload analysis
Nos of children, including number of births	maternity hospital returns, health visitor caseload
Employment Unemployment rates and trends	local DoE office, LA economic planning department
Types and patterns of local employment, e.g. full-time/ part-time work	local people, economic planning department
Wages patterns, e.g. people on low wages	economic planning departments, local knowledge
Health *Your local Annual Report of the Director of Public Health will contain much of the information listed here.*	
Incidence and rates of poverty-related ill health problems, e.g. respiratory problems due to damp	community nursing team, GPs, HA research and information dept
Immunisation up-take	health visitors, GPs, HA research and information dept
Rates of low birth weight babies	OPCS data, HVs, HA research and information dept
Death rates	OPCS data, HA research and information dept
Accident rates (home and road)	police, environmental health dept, HA information dept
Mental health problems	CPNs, SSD, local support groups, HVs
People with disabilities	referral/caseload analysis
Housing Tenure patterns Type of housing, e.g. terraced, flats etc. Housing conditions, e.g. overcrowding, damp, suitability for families, design	LA housing department, tenants' groups
Fuel and housing debts	caseload analysis, Citizens' Advice Bureau
Transport Availability of car, public transport to shops and essential services etc.	census (car ownership), local knowledge, bus company timetables and fares
Services (current and planned) *Local authority and health authority strategic plans and annual reports will be useful here.*	
Childcare and pre-school provision	SSD, HVs, local knowledge
Day care provision for older adults, people with physical and mental disabilities	SSD, Community nurses, voluntary organisations and groups
Carers' support	SSD, HA, voluntary groups
Availability of support services and use of services	SSD, HA, education dept, voluntary agencies
Local facilities (shops, recreational, and social)	local knowledge
Consumer satisfaction with services	consumer/user surveys, information gained at open meeting/forums

! Your team will need to identify the types of information that will be most useful to you. Team activity 4A will help you to work through the process of identifying information needs and collecting information for your poverty and health profile.

THINKING CRITICALLY: GUIDELINES FOR ANALYSING INFORMATION

The analysis stage of poverty profiling is concerned with 'making sense' of the information you have collected. The information you have collected will probably not appear to be very tidy: you will have a lot of data that you need to interpret. Do not be put off by this mass of information. The guidelines in this section will help you to make sense of it. A good way to work through the task of analysing information is to ask some questions about it. Below are some key questions for you to ask of your information.

Is the Information Accurate and Reliable?

• **Look behind, through and under the information to interpret what it means.** Information, particularly statistical data, can be misleading. It can often tell you more than one story, depending on how you look at it. For example, figures that tell you that only 10 people used your duty service, clinic or group last year could be interpreted as meaning that the service was not needed or that it was not used for reasons such as, it was at an inconvenient time or was difficult to use. Statistics also only give you a snapshot of what is happening at any one particular time. They may obscure what happens at particular times of the year, or in between snapshots. For example, in areas where employment is seasonal families may move in and out of poverty at particular times of the year.

• **Identify who collected the information and why.** Statistics may be collected to prove a particular point that someone wants to make. If this is the case they may not be telling the whole story.

• **Check whether the information is up-to-date.** If it is not, it may not be giving you

an accurate picture. Some information, such as the census, will inevitably be out of date. This does not mean that you should not use it – it may be the only source of information available to you. It means that you should use it with caution and look to see if and how circumstances have changed since the statistics were gathered.

• **Get a broader picture.** Talk to key people about the statistics. Key people may be able to tell you the picture behind the figures or give you an 'alternative' or 'unofficial' view of the figures. Some examples of key people to talk to are listed below:

* local people, including those in parents' groups, minority ethnic groups, residents' and tenants' groups
* women's groups
* youth groups
* isolated individuals or families
* local community workers
* the person/persons who collected the statistics
* local church leaders
* workers in the voluntary sector

People seem to think our kids keep having accidents because we have dangerous homes. Well, the truth of it is that they hurt themselves because they're locked inside all day..... Round here there isn't anywhere our kids can play outdoors, so we keep them in. I reckon it's better to risk letting my little 'uns hurt themselves inside than risk letting them get run over by a double decker bus!

(a mother's explanation of home accidents)

What Does the Information Tell Us?

• **Identify what the information tells you about who, what, where, when and how.** Who is in poverty? Which areas do they live in? Do poverty levels differ throughout the year? Whose health is affected and how?

• **Try to identify the significant factors that affect people's health and well-being:** for example, poor housing, the environment, lack of transport and poor health facilities.

• **Try to identify common patterns and trends in the neighbourhood.** This will help you to move from an individual analysis to a broader analysis and reduce the risk of individualising problems.

• **Try to identify possible links and relationships between common needs and problems.** For example, stress and depression among mothers may be associated with poor access to childcare facilities in a neighbourhood.

• **Try to identify the demand for and gaps in service provision.** Are services reaching those families with the greatest needs? Areas with high demands may not necessarily be those with the greatest need.

How Effective Are Your Current Fieldwork Strategies and Methods of Working?

• **Identify which needs are already being met and which are not being met by existing provision.**

It's OK if you're white round here, but if you're Indian like me, there isn't anything for us. Our kids really miss out.

(a father talking about neighbourhood facilities)

• **Try to identify whether your current goals, strategies and methods of practice have:**

* helped families to avoid the worst aspects of poverty?

* helped families cope with those aspects of poverty that are unavoidable?

* helped families to tackle those aspects of poverty which can be changed?

* where possible, tried to change any of the factors that create and maintain their poverty?

SECTION 4

61

- facilitate decision-making at area level, that is help your manager to determine your resource needs.
- take into consideration the audience who may see it: use language which can easily be understood; use positive rather than stigmatising images; decide whether it needs translating into other languages.
- facilitate up-dating: poverty and health profiles need to be up-dated on a regular basis. Make sure that the layout of your report enables you to up-date it easily. Try using loose leaf sheets in a ring file so that you can take out a sheet of out-dated information and replace it with a new one, or put information on a word processor.

* **Talk to local people about the local facts and figures.** Facts and figures are powerful tools which can give local people the power to challenge decisions taken about them and services and policies that affect them. They should have access to the information. You could leave copies of your profile in reception areas, give copies to local groups, publish key facts in a newsletter, or hold a meeting.

* **Talk to colleagues, managers and other agencies.** Use your information as a way of getting family poverty on to the agenda of other agencies. But remember the note of caution on page 53. Other people may use the information in a way that you had not intended. So before you give other people information, plan how you will do it. Present it in a way that emphasises what families do achieve in the face of adversity and the relationship between their needs and social and economic policies.

We have a lot of young, pregnant women living on the estate. Most of them move into the flats and maisonettes during their pregnancy. We had never really thought about the preparation for parenthood services we provide for these women until we sat down and talked about our neighbourhood profile. Although we knew that women from the estate didn't tend to come to our preparation for parenthood classes here at the clinic as often as women from the private housing estate, we didn't realise that the attendance figures were as low as they were until we analysed the attendance figures by geographical areas. We then started to think what this meant alongside the information we had about low birth weights, housing conditions, and the number of families on the estate who are on income support. We realised that we weren't providing any sort of preparation for parenthood service for people on the estate, even though they are the ones who have the lowest incomes in the neighbourhood and live in very poor housing conditions.

We put all our information together and used it to argue the case to get an extra health visitor. We needed someone who could work just on developing a parentcraft and antenatal programme that would be attractive to families on the estate and more responsive to their health needs. It took some time to get our manager to agree to this, but we now have the funding for an extra health visitor for one year. It's only a pilot project, but if the post is successful it could continue and be tried in other areas of the city.

(A health visitor working in an inner city area)

❗ Activity 4B will guide you through the process of analysing your poverty and health profile information while activity 4C will help you to work out how you will disseminate it.

Summary and Conclusion

The purpose of poverty and health profiles is to assist the process of planning and the development of services. Ultimately, information can be used to identify the need for new and/or different areas of work and service provision. Gaps in service provision occur not only because some services do not reach those in need, but also because services appropriate to the needs of families in poverty are not available. Families may want not only more of existing services, such as childcare provision, but different kinds of services from those that are available.

This section has examined the need to assess local poverty levels and poverty-related problems. It has looked at the value of developing a poverty and health profile as a tool for assessing family poverty. The poverty and health profile provides a picture or account of the poverty levels and poverty-related problems that families in your neighbourhood face. This picture or account is unique to the families that you work with. The section that follows will examine how the poverty and health profile you have developed can be used to plan and develop support strategies for families in poverty.

Reference

1   Orr, J., Luker, K. (1985). *Health Visiting.* Oxford, Blackwell Scientific Publications.

SECTION 4

PLANNING FOR CHANGE

Introduction

The previous section looked at the importance of building up an information base on family poverty and offered a set of guidelines for collecting information for a poverty and health profile. Once information for a poverty and health profile has been collected it can be analysed and used to aid planning and action in the area of family poverty. Below is a diagram which shows how information collection and analysis relate to each other to aid fieldwork planning and action.

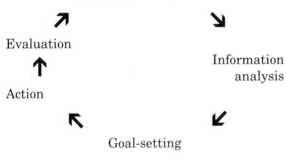

If you have followed the sections in this team training handbook and completed all the team activities, you will now be ready to use the information you have to set goals and objectives for the team.

Aims of the Section

i) to examine the key elements of responsive service provision for families in poverty;

ii) to identify how information from health profiles can be used to set goals and objectives for practice;

iii) to encourage workers to consider critically factors which influence organisations when planning services for families in poverty.

Team Activities

- 5A Clarifying roles
- 5B Deciding on goals and priorities

Information Sheets

- What are responsive services?
- What can workers do?
- Setting goals and objectives
- Organisational factors and planning for change

SECTION 5

Notes for Facilitator

Team activities 5A and 5B:

- Emphasise that these activities need to be considered as a planning exercise that will come up with goals for you to work towards in your daily practice. They are not just a paper exercise.

- If people are worried about the time it takes to carry out these activities, remind them that time spent now will pay off in the long term.

CLARIFYING ROLES

Estimated time: 75 mins
Method: individual and group work
Materials: copies of Roles Chart (page 67), flip chart and pens, copy of your poverty
and health profile

Relevant information sheets: *What are responsive services? What can workers do?*

This activity will help you to think about how you carry out monitoring, alleviating/preventing
and social change roles in your practice and to begin to think about how you need to extend or
change roles to make your practice more effective in the area of family poverty.

1   **Working as a group, brain-storm to identify the monitoring, alleviating/preventing
    and social change roles that the team has carried out over the last twelve months.
    Fill in column 1 of the chart.** (15 mins)

2   **Using your poverty and health profile, think about how you need to extend or
    change your monitoring, alleviating/preventing and social change roles to respond
    more effectively to the needs of local families in poverty:**
    –   begin by working individually and fill in column 2 of the chart. (10 mins)
    –   pool your individual ideas and produce a collective list. (20 mins)

3   **As a group, try to identify:** (total 30 mins)
    –   any factors which helped you to carry out these roles:
        e.g. *Our area manager / nursing officer encouraged a monitoring role.*
    –   any factors or tensions which have made it difficult to carry out these roles:
        e.g. *No interpreter was available for the Asian community.*
    –   how well equipped you feel to carry out these roles.
    –   any training, support or organisational changes that would enhance your ability to carry
        out these roles.

Action Point!

This activity will give you some indication of the broad roles that your team needs to
consider over the next 12 months. Keep a copy of your individual charts and collective list
and use it in the next activity.

ROLES CHART
(use with activity 5A)

Column 1 Roles carried out over last 12 months	Column 2 Roles needed in next 12 months
Monitoring: Alleviating / preventing: Social change:	Monitoring: Alleviating / preventing: Social change:

Team Activity 5B

DECIDING ON GOALS AND PRIORITIES

Estimated time: 1 day or two 1/2 day sessions
Method: individual and group work
Materials: flip chart, pens, copies of Goals Sheet (page 70) and
Team Action Plan (page 71)

Relevant information sheets: *What are responsive services? What can workers do? Setting goals and objectives; Organisational factors and planning for change*

This activity will help your team to work through the process of setting goals and objectives to guide your fieldwork practice with families in poverty. Use the chart you filled in for activity 5A to help you identify priority areas of work.

1 **Working individually and using the Goals Sheet attached to this activity, write down three goals that you think should be priority areas of work for the team concerning family poverty.** (10 mins)

2 **Working as a group, put together a composite list of possible goals and priorities. Ask your facilitator to write them on a flip chart. Individuals can extend their own lists by adding in the goals that other people identify.** (20 mins)

3 **As a group, evaluate whether you can justify the goals you have identified by asking the following questions:** (1–2 hours)

   i) What evidence is there to justify the goals and priorities identified?
       – hard facts? if so, from where? (e.g. your poverty and health profile, consumer survey, policy documents etc.)
       – assumptions and general expectations?
       – anecdotes?

   ii) Which goals are compatible with consumer opinion and agency goals and priorities?

   iii) To what extent are these goals compatible with/different from your current team goals/ priorities?

4 **Agree on a list of key goals for the team and place them in order of priority. Write them in the middle section of the Goals Sheet:** (1–2 hours)

   – It is probably not realistic to identify more than three goals at this stage.
   – Try to identify goals that are compatible with both consumer opinion and agency expectations. These are likely to be the easiest to achieve. Write them down in order of priority in the middle section of the Goals Sheet.

   * If you have goals that are not compatible with consumer or agency expectations, consider whether these are appropriate. If you still think they are, think about how you will justify them and discuss some of the difficulties that may arise.

SECTION 5

68

* You may want to keep a reserve list of goals and priorities. If you do, write this in the bottom section of the Goals Sheet.
* Note any disagreements between team members and discuss how you will handle and resolve any conflicts.

5   As a group, write a set of objectives for each goal: (1 – 2 hours)

i) Use a copy of the Action Plan (page 71) for each goal. Write your first goal in column 1 of the sheet.

ii) Identify a set of objectives that will enable you to attain each goal and write them in column 2 of the sheet.

iii) Only fill in the first two columns of the sheet at this stage. You can fill in the other columns when you have worked through the next section of the team training handbook.

Action Point!

Minute your collective list of goals and priorities. This is your team working agreement. It should form the basis of your team action plan in section 6.

GOALS SHEET
(use with activity 5B)

Individual goals

Agreed priority goals for team

Reserve list of goals

ACTION PLAN MATRIX
(use with activities 5B & 6B)

1 Goal	2 Objectives	3 Timescale	4 Target Groups	5 Method/s	6 Person/s Responsible

WHAT ARE RESPONSIVE SERVICES?

Family accounts of poverty, in addition to providing insights into the effect of poverty on family life, also provide a valuable bank of information on the types of health and welfare services and interventions that families find helpful. Family views about services need to form the basis of service planning and provision and are important to take into consideration when setting goals and objectives. This information sheet examines what type of provision families in poverty themselves identify as helpful and unhelpful.

What Type of Health and Welfare Responses do Families in Poverty Find Unhelpful?

* services that treat financial, health and social problems as unrelated;
* individual agencies working on separate sets of problems;
* only getting help when things are really bad;
* interventions that individualise problems;
* services that are based on what professionals think parents want rather than what parents themselves say they want;
* failure to recognise what parents do achieve in the face of adversity;
* blaming parents for their poverty;
* temporary and short term interventions/ projects to longer term difficulties;
* having to define financial problems as emotional problems or personal inadequacy to get help;
* only having access to help when someone has labelled the family as 'a problem' or 'cause for concern';

What Type of Health and Welfare Responses do Families Find Helpful?

Some common elements come out of family accounts of using health and welfare services in poverty. These are summarised below:

✓ **An integrated approach:** health and welfare responses that do not treat financial, health and social problems as separate entities. Families appreciate workers who recognise that poverty has health and social costs and that ill health has financial costs. And parents do not want to deal with three or four workers when they could deal with one.

✓ **A co-ordinated response from agencies:** individual agencies are working on common issues, using complementary approaches and providing services that are not duplicated but leave no gaps. Responses need to be co-ordinated within teams and agencies and across agencies. The process of co-ordinating responses at team and inter-agency levels will be examined in section 6.

✓ **Services that are permanent:** services that are available on a long-term basis. Short-term funding has led to a proliferation of services that are not permanent. For many families, very small-scale initiatives that are permanent are better than large-scale temporary services. Short-term projects often raise expectations that cannot be met in the long-term.

✓ **Partnership with workers:** parents and workers working together towards common goals. Partnership means valuing the contribution of families. Families are not passive recipients of care. They are the main providers of care and actively assume responsibility for this care on a daily basis. Evidence suggests that parents in poverty have the same attitudes to childcare and health, and want the same things for their children as other families.[1] While parents in poverty hold similar goals to other parents, their ability to reach them is confined by their access to material and social resources for health. Nor are parents passive in poverty. They seek to manage their poverty, and minimise the effects of poverty on family members. Parents appreciate workers who reflect this in the support they offer.

✓ **Realistic advice:** advice that is possible to implement within the limitations of low income. Parents in poverty want workers to recognise that they are just as knowledgeable about what constitutes good care (childcare, health care, healthy eating) as other families. They appreciate it when professionals recognise that advice often has monetary costs that are beyond the pocket of many low income families. 'Throw away the chip pan', 'take your child to play group', 'buy a stair gate' are all examples of advice that cost money and may be beyond the means of many families on low income. Families appreciate workers who consider carefully the effect that their advice will have on families and consider ways by which they can help families to off-set or minimise the cost. Safety equipment loan schemes, low-cost equipment purchase schemes and food co-operatives are examples of health and welfare responses that minimise material costs to low-income families.

✓ **Services that are easy to use:** services that are flexible and easy to use. Families in poverty often need to use services more frequently than other families, yet many parents find that the barriers – personal and material – to using services are too great. This is particularly the case for many Black and minority ethnic groups. Such families not only experience higher levels of poverty than equivalent white families, but they also experience language and cultural barriers, and personal and institutional racism in their relationships with workers and agencies providing services.

✓ **Services that are relevant:** parents want services which meet what parents define as their needs rather than what professionals think are their needs. This means listening to families, accepting what they themselves identify as their needs and concerns, and building mechanisms whereby families can be listened to at all levels of planning.

The clinic are now holding a baby clinic in the community centre once a week. It's much easier for me to get to clinic now – I've only got to nip round the corner instead of walking up the main road for 20 minutes. It's at a better time too. The health visitors did a survey and most people wanted a clinic between 12 and 2 o'clock – I think they were a bit shocked by this. I've usually done my shopping by this time, and I've still got plenty of time before I pick up the others from school at 3 pm. I feed the baby before I go, and I take some sandwiches for me. I usually stay for a chat, eat my sandwiches and have a cup of tea (we didn't get that at the main clinic!). Every so often the welfare rights worker comes in. He sorted out my housing benefit for me last week. So you see, I got three things in one – the baby checked, my benefit sorted and I managed to talk to other mums as well!

(A lone mother with three young children)

WHAT CAN WORKERS DO?

Before your team can identify a set of goals it is important to spend some time thinking about the scope and limits of your professional role. Do not worry if you find it difficult to think about what you can do as it is not an easy task! There are no simple recipes that can be applied uniformly across communities, agencies or teams. Your team and individual team members need to identify broad areas of work that are acceptable to you, the community in which you work, and the agency you work for. While there are no simple recipes, there are frameworks which can help you to work out which roles might be acceptable. This activity sheet introduces one framework that spells out three broad roles that are important in family poverty work. It looks at how these roles can be carried out at various levels of intervention (individual/family, neighbourhood, area and national).

A Framework for Thinking About Work in the Area of Family Poverty

The framework introduced here identifies three broad roles for practitioners who work with families in poverty.

- **Monitoring:** gathering and analysing information to assess the impact of poverty on families through:

* poverty and health profiling (see section 4);

* monitoring and evaluating the effectiveness of service provision (see section 7);

* monitoring how specific policies affect families (for example, the effect of the Social Fund and local authority charging policies).

Monitoring forms the basis of two further areas of work: alleviating/preventing and social change.

- **Alleviating and preventing:** helping families to avoid and alleviate the effects of poverty through:

* helping families to maximise income levels (for example, helping families to claim benefits, initiating benefit up-take campaigns);

* advocacy (for example, negotiating with fuel boards and DSS);

* improving access to services;

* minimising the financial and emotional costs of using services (for example, by offering them in easily accessible venues, at convenient times and in a format that is culturally and socially acceptable to different ethnic and social groups);

* providing information about services, particularly about how to use and get access to them;

* targeting resources at those with the greatest needs;

* providing support and working in partnership with individuals and groups.

- **Bringing about social change:** where possible, working for changes to team, local and national policies through:

* social comment: initiating discussions on how poverty affects family health and how policies can lock families into poverty;

* working for the development of policies that do not maintain or create family poverty (for example, local authority anti-poverty policies, improved childcare policies);

* the development of team and agency employment policies that do not keep employees in poverty (for example, through minimal use of short-term contracts, and

introduction of flexible working times/
patterns);
* transferring knowledge, skills and control
to local people so that they have the
information and resources to challenge the
social and economic causes of poverty
themselves.

Areas of Work and Levels of Intervention

Monitoring, alleviating/preventing and social
change can all be carried out at various levels
of intervention:
* **at individual and family level:** problems/
needs stemming from poverty can be
responded to on an individual or family
basis by workers;

* **at neighbourhood level:** common issues/
problems can be responded to across a
neighbourhood;
* **at agency or area level:** issues and
problems can be responded to through the
development of agency/area strategies.

> **A structural perspective on poverty suggests that responses need to be developed at more than one level of intervention.**

Below is a matrix that contains some
examples of how workers can carry out
monitoring, alleviating/preventing and social
change roles at various levels of intervention.

Levels of Intervention

Role	Individual	Neighbourhood	District / Area
Monitoring	• assessing and recording effects of poverty on the health and well-being of individuals and families	• building poverty and health profiles to monitor effects of poverty and policies across the neighbourhood • monitoring effects of service provision across the neighbourhood	• monitoring local poverty trends • comparing poverty levels between areas • monitoring the effects of local authority and health authority policies on poor families
Alleviating/ Preventing	• developing non-stigmatising service provision and methods of practice • making services easy to use and culturally relevant, especially for Black and minority ethnic families • helping families to maximise their incomes • developing anti-discriminatory practice in area of 'race', gender and disability	• working with residents and neighbourhood groups to identify appropriate service provision • assisting local groups to get access to seed funding for voluntary and community initiatives (food co-ops, credit unions, etc.) • welfare benefits uptake campaigns • working to develop more childcare places, holiday playschemes, etc. • working with other agencies and groups to integrate and co-ordinate provision	• contributing to the development of area policies to assist families in poverty • using neighbourhood information to argue for additional, or the reshaping of, services • working to develop area schemes, such as safety equipment loan schemes
Social Change	• using methods of practice that are empowering for clients • encouraging individuals to challenge social and economic polices, e.g. campaigns to increase child benefit	• supporting local pressure groups • commenting on how local policies affect the neighbourhood • working to ensure that housing benefit is paid on time	• challenging local policies that are not in the interests of poor families, for example, local authority charging policies • lobby local councillors about neighbourhood resources • using local trade unions or professional bodies to campaign for better agency employment policies, e.g. job shares, decent pay levels for low paid workers

It is also important to be aware of the national context of health and welfare work. Although responding at national level may be beyond your paid health and welfare role, it is possible to try to influence national policies in your professional and personal capacity. Some ways of doing this are:

* supporting anti-poverty groups (for example, Child Poverty Action Group);
* being active in your local professional organisation or trade union;
* trying to get family poverty on the agenda of your national professional organisations and trade unions;
* lobbying local MPs about the issues;
* writing to the press in a personal capacity or as a member of a professional body or trade union.

Some Key Questions That You May Want Answered

If the causes of poverty are structural, surely ameliorative responses are trivial, operating on the margins rather than on the roots of the problem?

The recognition that poverty is structural understandably raises questions in workers' minds about their ability to have any real influence on the problems that poor families face. However, there are no signs that the climate in which families care will change for the better in the near future. Families will continue to live in poverty. Sensitive, empowering responses at a time of continuing economic recession may be better than nothing. They can be combined with or form one part of a strategy concerned with change.

Aren't health and welfare workers, in reality, only the new rationers of poor relief?

Health and welfare workers clearly exercise some control over the distribution of health and welfare resources, mediating family access to vital services. Government policies have sought to strengthen this role in recent years,

for example by requiring workers to co-operate in the process of determining who should and who should not have access to community care grants. Whilst this role inevitably causes tensions, it can be used to the advantage of families. Workers can ensure that those groups who often have the most difficulty getting access to resources are supported.

Some Key Points

• It is important to monitor conditions, support families, prevent harm and evaluate services if a structural perspective is to be reflected in practice responses.

• For strategies to be effective, you need to work at more than one level of intervention in your work with families.

• When working at an individual/family level it is important to recognise that different family members are not affected uniformly by poverty. The support/advice/services you offer or recommend may be in the interests of one family member but not in the interests of another.

• All team members need to be involved in the work, including receptionists and care assistants – not only front-line workers.

• You need to check out whether your job description allows you to carry out monitoring, alleviating/preventing and social change roles. If not, you will need to work to establish maximum flexibility in job descriptions.

Role definitions and job descriptions

Role perceptions and the scope to carry out particular roles are shaped by agency policies, particularly in the statutory field. Some job descriptions are broad enough to allow workers to adopt all of the roles described in this information sheet, others are not. It may be necessary to negotiate tensions between your professional responsibility to ensure the best possible service for clients and agency or political expectations. You could do this by:

* pointing out how existing policies and legislation (for example, local anti-poverty policies or the Children Act (1989)) identify a requirement to respond to family poverty;

* enlisting your trade union or professional body to help your team to negotiate any tensions with your agency;

* if your team or team leader is involved in writing a job description for a new member of staff, making sure that it will allow the adoption of monitoring, alleviating/preventing and social change roles.

While wider job descriptions can aid team functioning, it is important to ensure that they do not lead to exploitation of team members, particularly people in low-grade and low-paid jobs.[2] Broadening people's job descriptions can mean that they are required to take on more responsibility or tasks that they are not qualified to do without any increase in pay or status.

! Activity 5A provides a framework for you to think about the monitoring, alleviating/preventing and social change roles you have carried out over the past 12 months and to evaluate if and how these need to change or be extended.

SETTING GOALS AND OBJECTIVES

This information sheet examines both the process of setting goals and objectives and also those factors which need to be taken into account when setting goals and objectives to direct your work with families in poverty.

What Are Goals and Objectives?

• **A goal** is a broad statement of intention. For example:

– to reduce the number of home accidents in the neighbourhood;

– to promote user input into service planning;

– to improve support for depressed and isolated parents.

Each goal usually has a list of objectives or sub-goals.

• **An objective** represents an initial specification of the activities and strategies the team will use in order to achieve the main goal:[3]

– to set up a user group to provide feedback on service provision;

– to provide a drop-in facility for parents under stress;

– to organise an action group to improve pre-school provision;

– to assist Black parents to set up a support group.

Setting goals and objectives for fieldwork practice with families makes a statement about your values and priorities in working with families in poverty.

Goals and objectives to direct health and welfare strategies for family poverty essentially reflect choices about:

* priorities: family poverty issues/problems you intend to respond to;

* groups you intend to work with: client groups, neighbourhood groups and other workers;

* the process: how you will achieve goals.

Choices need to be based on a process of needs assessment and active goal-setting.

Why Set Goals and Objectives?

* It is not possible to respond to all needs and demands: there is not the time, energy or resources;

* They help workers to make a purposeful choice about their work;

* They help to focus practice;

* They enable the development of an integrated team policy;

* They can help workers avoid 'burn out': realistic goal-setting should make workloads appear more manageable and make managers and other agencies aware of what you can and cannot do;

* Goal-setting is essential to the idea of evaluation: it is necessary to have some statement of intention by which outcomes can be evaluated.

Using information from poverty and health profiles to set goals is one way of putting poverty on the central agenda of local fieldwork practice.

Some Key Points About Goals and Objectives

- **They should be based on an assessment of local poverty levels and family support needs.** Using your poverty and health profiles to set goals will mean that goals are based on facts rather than intuition, hear say and untested assumptions.

- **They need to be appropriate at different levels of intervention, drawing on models which ensure responsiveness to consumers** (see section 6).

- **They need to be realistic and achievable.** Setting unrealistic goals and objectives will lead to feelings of failure and loss of motivation. Realistic goals encourage you to identify and specify to yourselves, your managers, local people and other agencies what you can and cannot achieve. The next information sheet in this section examines some of the organisational factors that you will also need to take into account.

- **They need to be pro-active.** Despite the harsh political climate, opportunities still exist for workers to be pro-active, that is, help families to avoid some of the financial, material and social crises that are a common part of daily life in poverty. Pro-active responses require workers to think about how they can move away from crisis responses towards preventive responses.

! Team activity sheet 5B will help your team to set about the process of setting goals and objectives for practice. However, before you move on to this activity you will need to consider some of the organisational factors that may constrain goal- and objective-setting. The next information sheet examines some of the organisational factors that you will need to take into account.

ORGANISATIONAL FACTORS AND PLANNING FOR CHANGE

A number of organisational factors are likely to influence goal- and objective-setting at team level. This information sheet examines some of the factors that need to be taken into account.

Why Consider Organisational Factors?

* They can be enabling or constraining factors for neighbourhood teams, depending on local circumstances and the nature of the response being considered by the team.

* Failure to give due attention to these factors can lead to goals and objectives that are inappropriate and unrealistic.

* Working on issues of family poverty is fraught with organisational constraints. It is less stressful and more effective to be clear about what they are than to ignore them.

Failure to consider organisational factors can mean the planning process collapses. On the other hand, taking such factors into consideration may leave teams feeling that they are unable to move forward. Although it is vital to accept that these factors are 'real', this does not necessarily mean that all constraints should be accepted without question. Some agency mandates, goals, attitudes and resource allocations may be open to challenge.

It is important to analyse which organisational factors are negotiable or open to challenge and which must be accepted as unchangeable at a particular moment in time.

Some Organisational Factors to Take Into Account

To a large extent, the organisational factors that you will need to consider depend on local circumstances, particularly how local agencies have responded to government legislation and policies. Some of the general factors that you will need to consider are described below.

• **Organisational mandates.** These stem from government policies and legislation. Current legislation and policies shaping the mandates of health and welfare agencies include the Children Act (1989), National Health Service and Community Care Act (1990), General Practitioner contracts, Education Reform Act (1987) and the Social Security Act (1986). Mandates laid down by governments reflect a government's view about family and state responsibilities for health and welfare and the cause of social and economic problems. They are likely to be difficult to negotiate. While workers frequently find that some of this legislation constrains their work in the area of family poverty, it is possible to identify parts of the legislation that could be used to legitimise pro-active work with families in poverty. For example, under the Children Act (1989), Section 17, it can be argued that children living in poverty and at risk of family breakdown can be regarded as 'children in need' and hence entitled to family support services.[4] Although this Act places duties on local authorities and its staff, health workers may be the first to identify 'children in need' and have a key role to play in assessing the needs of children and promoting their welfare. Sections of this Act, therefore, could be used by both local authority workers and health workers to support pro-active team strategies in the area of family poverty.

> **It is important to ask of legislation 'how can we use it to support and legitimise our work with families in poverty?'**

• **Organisational goals and policies.** These are likely to reflect national and local government political attitudes to poverty, as well as mandates from government. Teams need to examine whether the goals they set fall into line with organisational policy, which may not acknowledge poverty as a central issue for service provision. Those workers within organisations that have anti-poverty policies are likely to be able to use these policies to legitimise their own goals and argue for resources to meet them. Others may need to look imaginatively at policy statements which may back up their analysis and commitments.

• **Resource allocation.** Cuts in public expenditure have reduced staffing levels and financial resources in many agencies at a time when demands on agencies have increased. However, it is also important to recognise that not all team strategies will require more resources. Recognising ways of using more effectively the time and skills of team members, volunteers, community resources and support networks and other agencies, as well as financial resources, can make a difference.

> **Whether time and resources act as constraining factors depends on the type of response being considered.**

* Responses may not require extra time or resources, for example, acknowledging the structural nature and experience of poverty in all interactions with families.

* Responses may require the reallocation of resources rather than additional resources, for example, using existing resources to set up a self help group rather than using them to help families on an individual basis.

* Responses may demand extra time and material resources in the short-term but save time and resources in the long-term. For example, setting up a support group for parents on low income or increasing the number of childcare places in a locality to save child protection resources in the long term.

* Some responses will have long-term resource costs which may not be off-set in the future, for example, the employment of an additional team member.

Challenging Constraints

Below are some ways in which you, individually and as a team, may be able to challenge organisational constraints.

* Lobby policy makers (e.g. local MPs and councillors, government ministers, managers) about the need for policies that tackle family poverty, improve family health and do not lock certain social groups into disadvantage.

* Argue the case for more or different resources for the team.

* Make applications for grants to support new areas of work. You could consider applying for funds from voluntary organisations, local businesses, the Church Urban Fund or Urban Aid monies.

* Use professional organisations and trade unions to highlight the importance of poverty and health issues for practice and the need for social policies that reduce family poverty and improve family health.

* Support the work of anti-poverty groups and groups who work for the welfare of families (e.g. Child Poverty Action Group, National Council for One Parent Families and the Maternity Alliance).

* Find out how legislation can be used to put pressure on policy makers. For example, the Children Act (1989) places a general duty on local authorities to safeguard and promote the health and welfare of children in need and to promote the upbringing of such children by their families. You could use the information in your profile to indicate where provision is needed if local authorities are to meet their responsibilities or to indicate where they are failing to do so.

* Support local groups who are campaigning for better resources and services for families. For example, you could provide a room for them to meet in and the use of photocopying equipment, offer assertiveness training and skills training, help them to get access to decision-makers or provide them with statistical information to support their case.

* do not ask for the earth: show that you are aware that the agency purse is finite;
* anticipate counter-arguments and prepare replies to them;
* where possible, show how the work you plan to do fits in with your organisation's mandate and policies.

Arguing the case for resources

If you need to put forward a case for more or different resources, it is important to develop a coherent and logical argument:

* think through and rehearse your arguments;
* get your facts straight;
* use information from your poverty and health profile to highlight the extent of the problem;
* use research data to back up your arguments;
* be clear about what you would use any additional resources for, both in the short-term and the long-term;
* use language that does not appear to be too political to budget holders: some managers dislike the connotations of words like 'structural';[5]

Summary and Conclusion

This section has examined the 'planning for change' stage in the process of building responsive support strategies for families in poverty. It has examined the key elements of responsive service provision. It also looked at how information from poverty and health profiles can be analysed and used to set goals and objectives for practice.

The section has emphasised the need for workers to carry out three key roles in their practice: a monitoring role, an alleviating/ preventing role, and a social change role. It has stressed the need for workers to think about these roles at three levels of intervention: the individual/family level, neighbourhood level and area level, and the need to consider the national context within which health and welfare work takes place. The team activities have provided an opportunity to identify goals and objectives for practice, using a structural perspective on poverty and health. The next section moves on to look critically at the contribution that various methods of practice make to working on issues of family poverty, and the value of working in partnership with other agencies. The next section will enable you to complete your team action plan.

References and Notes

1 See Blackburn, C. (1991). *Poverty and Health: Working with Families.* Chapter 6, 'Caring for Children's Health in Poverty'. Buckingham, Open University Press.

2 Hadley, R., Cooper, M., Dale, P., Stacy, G. (1987). *A Community Social Worker's Handbook.* London, Tavistock Publications.

3 Henderson, P., Thomas, D. (1980). *Skills in Neighbourhood Work.* National Institute for Social Work. London, Allen and Unwin.

4 There are several publications that offer commentaries on and easy reference to the relevant sections of the Children Act (1989). See section 8 for references.

5 Dhooge, Y., Becker, S. (1989). *Working with Unemployment and Poverty: A Training Manual for Social Services.* London, South Bank Polytechnic.

SECTION 5

ENGAGING WITH FAMILIES AND OTHER WORKERS

Introduction

Setting goals and objectives, that is, deciding what to do, needs to be followed by the process of deciding how to do it. This section is concerned with this aspect of planning and building services for families in poverty.

The section begins by discussing how workers can and do respond to family poverty, examining critically the contribution that various methods make to family work and tackling family poverty. It then moves on to look at the value of working in partnership with other agencies and groups and the need to examine what team strategies mean for individual practice. The team activities in this section will help your team to identify possible partners to collaborate with, to define your team and individual training needs and to complete the team action plan matrix in section 5.

Aims of Section

i) to encourage workers to examine critically the methods they currently use, and could use to tackle family poverty;

ii) to examine the contribution of collaborative work in the area of family poverty;

iii) to explore the implications of team strategies for team and individual training needs.

Team Activities

- 6A   Identifying partners
- 6B   Completing the team action plan
- 6C   Identifying personal changes
- 6D   Identifying training needs

Information Sheets

- Looking at methods
- Working with other agencies and groups
- Translating team strategies into individual practice

Notes for Facilitator

Activity 6B:

- Completing the action plan is a core activity demanding time to build a realistic plan. You should stress that it is important to allocate enough time, adding additional sessions if needed.

Activity 6C:

- It is suggested that the first part of this activity is completed by individuals before the session. You should ask them at least a week in advance to do this work, ensuring that they are clear about the instructions.

- In this activity the term 'support' refers to mutual encouragement, time to talk through any problems and reassurance rather than material support (resources).

Team Activity 6A

IDENTIFYING PARTNERS

Estimated time: 90 mins
Method: group work
Materials: copies of Identifying Partners Matrix (page 87)

Relevant information sheet: *Working with other agencies and groups*

This activity will help you to think about who you could collaborate with on family poverty issues. The information you identify here will be useful in the next activity.

Work as a group throughout this activity:

1 (10 mins)
   i) **Examine the goals in your action plan. List them along the top of the matrix (you will need to write your goals in a shorthand form).**
   ii) **Tick from the list on the left-hand side of the Identifying Partners Matrix, the key groups and agencies that could help you to achieve your goals. Add in any other groups that you can think of.**

2 (30 mins)
   i) **Identify named workers or key people within these agencies/groups to approach to begin discussions about collaborative work. Discuss what the nature of this contact should be (for example, what will you raise with them, offer to them or ask of them?).**
   ii) **You may already have contact with some of these groups, if so, identify whether this contact needs to be changed or extended, and if so, how.**
   iii) **Negotiate which member/s of the team will undertake this liaison work.**

3 **Identify whether there is any existing formal liaison machinery (for example, local forums) to help groups and agencies to develop an integrated response. If there is, discuss how you could use it. If there is not, discuss whether you could think about developing a liaison network. If you do decide to develop a liaison network agree a date to discuss this further, possibly at your next regular team meeting.** (30 mins)

4 **Identify, in the light of this discussion, whether you need to change any of your goals and priorities identified in activity 5B. If so, amend your team action plan.** (20 mins)

IDENTIFYING PARTNERS MATRIX
(use with activity 6A)

Groups	Goals		
• health visitors			
• social workers			
• nursery workers			
• playgroup workers			
• community workers			
• community education workers			
• teachers			
• welfare rights workers			
• midwives			
• district nurses			
• general practitioners			
• police			
• library staff			
• local church people			
• councillors			
• tenants' groups			
• community groups			
• voluntary project workers			
• campaign groups			
•			
•			
•			
•			

COMPLETING THE TEAM ACTION PLAN

Estimated time: 3 hours or a 1/2 day
Method: group work
Materials: copies of the Team Action Plan Matrix (page 71)

Relevant information sheet: *Looking at methods*

This activity links with activity 5B. It provides an opportunity for you to complete the Team Action Plan Matrix you began in activity 5B (page 71) by filling in the timescale, the target groups, methods and 'who does what' columns.

Use the Team Action Plan Matrix and work as a group throughout this activity:

1   **Identify a realistic timescale for each objective. Some goals will have both long-term and short-term objectives. Write the timescales in column 3 of the Team Action Plan Matrix.** (30 mins)

2   **Identify the target groups for each objective. Remember that target groups can be client and non-client groups (some of the partners you identified in activity 6A). Write them in column 4 of the Team Action Plan Matrix.** (20 mins)

3   **Identify which methods are most appropriate and will help you to achieve your goals and objectives. Write them in column 5 of the Team Action Plan Matrix.** (40 mins)

4   **Decide which team members will be responsible for which objectives. Make sure you take into consideration the various skills of individual team members – do not necessarily stick to traditional divisions of labour. Fill in column 6 of the Team Action Plan Matrix.** (40 mins)

5   **Identify what revisions need to be made to existing workload allocations and record this. Ask your facilitator to record this decision, have it typed and circulated to the team so you all have a written record of any decisions.** (40 mins)

6   **Decide who needs to be consulted/informed of your revised team strategy and workload changes (for example, your manager or administrative staff) and who will carry out this task.** (10 mins)

IDENTIFYING PERSONAL CHANGES

Estimated time: 80 mins
Method: individual work, work in pairs, group work
Materials: copies of Personal Changes Chart (page 91)

Relevant information sheets: *Looking at methods, Translating team strategies into individual practice.*

This activity will help you to work out what the team action plan means for your practice as individuals within the team. It will help you to identify what changes you need to make to what you do and how you do it. It will save time if you complete the first and second boxes of the Personal Changes Chart **before** you come to the session.

> **Over the week preceding this session,** look at each goal and corresponding plan of action:
>
> i) think about what each part of the team action plan means for what you each do as individuals in your daily work. Fill in box 1 of the chart.
>
> ii) think about what each part of the team action plan means for how you carry out your activities. Fill in box 2 of the chart.

1   **In pairs, take 20 minutes each to discuss what you wrote in the first and second boxes of the chart. As each person discusses her/his individual practice, the other person in the pair can ask some questions that will help the speaker to check out:**

   i)   that s/he has considered as many aspects of daily practice as possible, in particular issues of 'race', gender and disability. Some questions that could be asked include:

   How will you enable all clients to be more involved in decisions that affect their daily lives?

   How will you check out that Black and minority ethnic families find your practice ethnically sensitive?

   How will you work with women so that your practice does not compound the gender and racial inequalities that lock them into poverty and disadvantage?

   ii) what support s/he will need to make any changes. Write any support needs identified in box 3 of the chart.

2   **As a group, take it in turns to:** (40 mins)

   i)   share the changes that you, as individuals, feel you need to make;

   ii) any concerns you have and the support you feel you need to carry out these changes;

   iii) try to identify which support needs can be met and how you will meet them.

   e.g.   *We will allocate 10 mins at the end of each team meeting to discuss how we are progressing. We could pair up to offer each other support.*

Action Points!

* If you have identified that you need support from outside the group, identify a person/s to seek out this support on behalf of the group.

* If you have identified that some of your support needs are unlikely to be met, make a note of these and make sure that your manager is informed.

IDENTIFYING PERSONAL CHANGES CHART
(use with activity 6C)

Box 1: What I do
What I need to change: What I do well and do not need to change: What I need to do more of:

Box 2: The methods I use
What I need to change: What I do well and do not need to change: What I need to do more of:

Box 3: The support I need to make the above changes

Team Activity 6D

IDENTIFYING TRAINING NEEDS

Estimated time: 1 hour
Method: brain-storm, individual work and group discussion
Materials: flip chart, pens, copies of Training Needs Chart (page 93) for each team
member. Ask individuals to bring their own Identifying Personal Changes
Chart (from activity 6C).

Relevant information sheet: *Translating team strategies into individual practice*

This activity will help you to identify any training you will need as individuals and as a team, to enable you to carry out your action plan.

1   **As a group, brain-storm to identify the skills and knowledge you will need to carry out your action plan. Draw on your team action plan matrix to do this. Ask your facilitator to write them on a flip chart. Individuals can fill them in on their own Training Needs Charts.**

2   **Working individually, go down the list and tick the skills and knowledge you feel confident in and put a cross by those that you need some further training in.**

3   **As a group, identify the training needs that are common to the whole or the majority of the team. Identify the most urgent needs (not more than two) and those that need to be considered in the future. Write these in the middle section of the Training Needs Chart.**

4   **Working individually, make a list of your own priority training needs that cannot be met within the team training programme and write them in the bottom section of the Training Needs Chart. Refer back to activity 6C and box 3 of your Identifying Personal Changes Chart to see whether you have any additional training needs arising from the changes you wish to make in your own practice. Enter these in the bottom section of the chart.**

Action Points!

*   Identify a team member/s to be responsible for setting up and co-ordinating a training programme.

*   As individuals, bring your personal training needs to the attention of your manager or team leader. Your next supervision session or staff appraisal session may be a suitable opportunity to do this. If not, make an appointment to do so.

TRAINING NEEDS CHART
(use with activity 6D)

Skills / knowledge	Individual needs	Team needs

Top team training needs	Lower priority training needs

Individual Training Needs

LOOKING AT METHODS

Workers use a variety of methods in their work with families. The 'method' is the form that practice takes, the way that workers go about achieving their goals. Thinking about and deciding on methods, therefore, is a key part of building responsive strategies for families in poverty.

> **Whether your team is able to reach the goals you set in the last section depends on whether you choose the right methods.**

Before you build your action plan it is useful to examine what each method has to offer to family support work. This information sheet will look at the methods that workers can and do use in their work with families in poverty.

Methods of Practice

There are three broad methods of responding in health and welfare work:

*   one-to-one method: one worker working with an individual or family;

*   group work method: one or more workers working with a group of clients or people from the neighbourhood;

*   community development method: encouraging local people to define their own needs and join together to bring about change in service provision or their social circumstances.

Different staff groups within the broad category of health and welfare work use each of the three methods to varying degrees. Workers use different methods because they often have different goals. However, it is also important to remember that choice of method depends on other factors including:

*   what people think their role should be
*   the historical development of professions
*   agency expectations
*   previous experience
*   what workers feel skilled and comfortable in doing

The next sub-section looks at some of the pros and cons of different methods of practice. This information sheet does not intend to discuss each method in any depth, but rather to give a flavour of the potential and limitations of three common methods of practice in family poverty work.

One-to-One Method

Key features:

*   it involves an individual practitioner working with an individual or family;
*   it often concentrates on the mother as the key person in the family;
*   practitioners often only work with those individuals they have records for;
*   it is the most common method used in family work.

Contribution to work with families in poverty:

*   it is a method by which workers can offer families close individual support;
*   it allows responses to be tailor-made to the needs of individuals or families;
*   it is essential when families need help at times of crises;

* it can be used to help individual families to negotiate access to other services and material resources;
* it can offer particular forms of help to families that cannot be provided by family, friends or the wider social support network, for example, with particular health problems, debt problems and problems that are stigmatising within the community.

Problems with this method:

* it can pathologise people or individualise problems that result from structural causes;

* it tends to be a reactive method of practice;

* it is frequently associated with practice that attempts to change the behaviour and attitudes of the individual or family;

* it cannot, on its own, challenge the factors that create or maintain poverty;

* it is very time-consuming;

* it can fail to recognise or respond to the tensions between the needs of different family members.

Group Work Method

Key features:
* it involves one or more workers working with a group of people;

* group members are active participants;

* the emphasis is usually on sharing and co-operation between group members and working towards common goals.

Contribution to work with families in poverty:
* it enables people in poverty with similar problems, concerns or interests to come together and support each other;

* it can be a way by which local people can attempt to challenge local factors that create or maintain poverty;

* it can be more cost-effective in time and resources than one-to-one work in the long term;

* it can be an alternative to professional intervention: it is a method which can encourage mutual aid and self help.

Problems with this method:

* it may be no more than an individual model of practice at the level of the group;

* it can be concerned with individual attitude and behaviour change through group processes;

* it is not necessarily empowering for group members: workers can retain control and power over the group.

Community Development Method

Key features:
* an individual or team of workers working at the level of the neighbourhood as a whole rather than its constituent parts;

* it is concerned with groups and networks rather than individuals or families;

* it involves a collective approach: individuals joining together to take collective action;

* health and well-being are seen as determined by the social context in which people live;

* it involves the community defining its own needs.

Contribution to work with families in poverty:
* it is the most appropriate method for developing responses at the neighbourhood level;

* it goes beyond the confines of individual and family work to analyse issues at the level of the community;

* it sees families as able to manage their own needs rather than as problematic;

* it actively involves the community in decision-making and goal-setting.

Problems with this approach:

* it does not necessarily provide support that meets the needs of individual families;
* neighbourhoods and families that have been disadvantaged for long periods may lack the confidence and skills to be actively involved in community action;
* residents do not necessarily form a cohesive group, therefore may not want to join together in collective action;
* it can raise expectations that cannot be met, leaving people feeling more dissatisfied and helpless.

Which Method?

It is important to realise that all methods of practice can be problematic! Different methods of practice are appropriate for different types of work. The method is simply the process by which workers attempt to achieve particular things. Each method has its place in health and welfare work.

There is a tendency for group work and community development methods to be seen as less legitimate activities, as optional extras to be added on if there is time. Group work and community development methods need to be seen as complementary and equally important methods of responding to family poverty as individual work.

> If poverty is to be responded to at a number of levels, then a variety of methods will be needed.

Criticisms of health and welfare responses to family poverty result not from problems implicit in the methods themselves but from:

* the use of inappropriate methods for the job;
* the content of the intervention rather than the method itself;
* failure to use a range of methods.

Key Points About Methods

* **Decide which type of activity you want to develop and then decide on a method or methods.** Some methods will be more effective than others in terms of carrying out monitoring, supporting, preventing or social change roles.

* **Be creative!** Do not be tempted to stick to the methods you usually use, just because they are familiar. Could you bring isolated parents together in a group rather than provide support on an individual basis? Would it be more effective to work with other workers and residents to set up a holiday play scheme and an after school club rather than warn parents on an individual basis about the dangers of letting children play out on the street?

* **Pay attention to the content of your intervention as well as the method:** all methods can be equated with an individual pathology model or a social change model, depending on the content of the intervention.

* **Re-examine the methods you use on a daily basis:** are they enabling you and your clients to achieve what you want to achieve?

* **Ensure that partnership is a key element of all methods:** with clients, local people, colleagues, and other agency workers.

* **Identify your training needs:** do you need to arrange some group work or community work training, or do you need to develop your skills in working in partnership with individual clients?

* **Check out what your clients think about the methods you use:** some people may prefer to meet together as a group to get support on a particular issue instead of seeing you individually, while others may prefer you to spend your time helping them to get funding to set up a play group rather than attend your behaviour management course for parents!

! Team activity 6B will help you to identify the
■ methods of practice that the team needs to
employ to meet its goals, while team activity
6C provides an opportunity for you, as
individuals, to work out what changes you
need to make in your own practice.

The pages that follow contain two examples of
practice, written by practitioners who have
worked extensively with families in poverty.
The first example, by Ann Rowe and Kate
Billingham, illustrates how group work can be
used creatively to support parents in poverty.
The second example, by Norma Baldwin and
Lyn Carruthers, shows how community
development work can provide an opportunity
for local people to influence the shape and
style of local services and help local workers to
build responsive and integrated services in a
neighbourhood for families in poverty.

45, COPE STREET

For the past five years a team of two health visitors, a midwife and two nursery nurses have been working at Cope Street in a rented house in an inner city area of Nottingham. Funded by the Community Unit of Nottingham Health Authority the team have been running groups for local young mothers with the aim of developing parenting skills and increasing health knowledge. We have run many different groups including: young mothers' groups, 'stand up for yourself', a group for parents of Black and mixed race children and more recently, a course to enable some of the young women to undertake home visiting to other newly referred young mothers.

Nearly all of the women who attend Cope Street undertake parenting in difficult circumstances: as unsupported mothers on Income Support, living in poor housing and lacking access to childcare facilities. We have learnt a great deal from the mothers and are now able to offer a service that is appropriate to the needs of young families living in poverty. The parents we work with have a great deal of knowledge and experience already. What they lack are the resources to apply their knowledge. Our approach is to raise awareness that poverty is not the fault of individuals whilst enabling them to find ways of working within it. We recognise the complexities surrounding health behaviour and parenting but we have learnt that certain preconditions need to be met if our work is to be effective:

1   Parents must identify their own needs and participate fully in the planning, content and evaluation of the work. At Cope Street, people decide what they want, choose the topics for group discussion and, through regular reviews, assess whether their needs have been met.

2   People need the opportunity to get together with others in the same situation as themselves to share experiences and to learn from each other. Any knowledge gained in this way will be relevant and applicable to their everyday lives.

3   Self-confidence. Without it change is not possible. We see groupwork as the most effective way of developing self-confidence as mothers can recognise their own and each other's skills, share their experiences in a safe environment and can exercise collective power that is not possible in a one-to-one situation with a health professional.

4   Accessibility to services. Many families find access to the health service difficult. In our antenatal sessions the women test their own urine, learn to use a fetal heart monitor and draw up their own programme for the group. We hope that our shared care approach develops their confidence when dealing with the health service. The training of young mothers to undertake home visits to new referrals has made Cope Street more accessible as these mothers are able to 'get alongside' other mothers in a way that health professionals are never able to.

Because our work is rooted in the experience of the women who use us, poverty is always on the agenda. In the group activities inequalities in health are frequently discussed whether in terms of gender, race or social class and the discussions always take account of the limited resources available to the women. We have also had to recognise that seemingly unhealthy behaviours such as smoking are important coping strategies for many parents living in poverty.

For us this work has not always been easy. Our advantaged economic position can make discussions of poverty uncomfortable and the collective strength of a group of young mothers takes some getting used to for health workers who are used to working one to one! However, we cannot ignore these issues if our service is to be effective, accessible and appropriate to families living in poverty.

Ann Rowe
(health visitor) and Kate Billingham
(professional development worker),
Nottingham Health Authority

HENLEY SAFE CHILDREN PROJECT

This is a project which aims to develop a neighbourhood support approach to families with young children in an area with extensive family poverty and high child-protection referrals.

The project arose following research into the numbers of children on the child protection register from different neighbourhoods. Two areas of the city, both with large council estates, stood out with much higher than average referral rates. One of them, with 12.4 per cent of the City's children, accounted for 24.8 per cent of children on the City's child protection register in 1989 and 22.6 per cent of children in 1991. It was noticeable that there were clusters of referrals from certain parts of the neighbourhood.

Two-thirds of the families in the area have low incomes and are in receipt of housing benefit or entirely dependent on state benefits. Statistics also show higher than average numbers of low birth weight babies, of other health problems and of children's accidents.

Discussions were held between professionals working in Social Services, Health, Education, Probation, NSPCC and other voluntary agencies and groups involving residents in the area about the need for preventive, supportive work. Funding was obtained from the Home Office Safer Cities project to employ a development worker in the neighbourhood for eighteen months or two years.

The project uses a partnership model – of professionals and local people – seeing parents and young people as experts on their own situation. The worker is focusing on parents' strategies for keeping their children safe and healthy, as well as their major sources of stress in bringing up their children in an area of poverty and disadvantage, rather than on so-called predictors of abuse and neglect within families. The worker has four main tasks:

* to talk and listen to parents with young children about: their successes and difficulties when bringing up children; ways they can help and support each other; how local services might best meet their and their children's needs.

* to ensure that parents and local residents participate fully in discussions about the direction and progress of the project; using a community development approach to enable the local community to act as a valuable source of information, expertise and advice.

* to liaise effectively with workers within the local statutory and voluntary sectors; to look in detail with them at what experiences and views of parents mean for services in the area; to listen to their views on priorities for parents and children and identify and try to fill gaps in local service provision.

* to ensure effective channels of communication and information are set up, to allow a two-way exchange of information and discussion of issues between parents and workers within local service provision.

It is hoped that local people will see the project as providing an opportunity to influence the shape and style of local services, and to do something about the common perceptions, expressed by one local mother:

There was nothing there for me when I needed it.

**Norma Baldwin and Lyn Carruthers,
Henley Safe Children Project
(Coventry NSPCC/University of Warwick)**

WORKING WITH OTHER AGENCIES AND GROUPS

Collaboration and partnership with other workers and groups are important aspects of developing responses to family poverty. Responses need to be integrated and co-ordinated, not only within agency teams but across agency teams and groups. This information sheet looks at the value of, problems with and types of collaborative work, and lists some key points to guide practice.

Why Collaborate With Other Agencies and Groups?

* It can generate new ideas and projects to support families in poverty.
* It can achieve things that are beyond the scope of a single agency, challenging policies that create and maintain poverty.
* It can lead to a better understanding of poverty-related problems in the neighbourhood, through the sharing of knowledge and information.
* It can lead to greater trust between residents and workers.
* It can lead to a co-ordinated and integrated support strategy for families
* It can save resources or lead to a better use of existing resources through avoiding duplication of services.
* It may generate new resources: some grants will only be given for shared initiatives.
* It can reduce stress: agency teams can receive valuable support and encouragement from other agencies and groups.
* It can put teams in contact with informal care networks – alternative resources that they would not normally make contact with.

Some Examples of Collaborative Work

* Joint research.
* Joint training and staff development programmes.
* Co-working: with individual families or groups.
* Joint provision of services: for example, social workers, health visitors and community nurses jointly staffing a drop-in facility for carers.
* Collaboration on planning: for example, joint planning a support strategy for Black parents.
* Local forums: workers' forums, agency heads' forums, or neighbourhood forums involving residents, workers, managers and councillors.
* Joint poverty profiling and community studies.
* Joint campaigning: for example, on the inadequacy of welfare benefits or to improve benefit uptake.

Who Could You Work With?

* social service teams
* health visiting teams
* local housing officers
* nursery, playgroup and crèche workers
* community education teams
* teachers from the local schools
* community nursing teams
* community psychiatric nurses
* local church people
* community workers and community centre users

* voluntary project workers
* local groups such as tenants' or residents' associations and community associations
* family centre teams
* local doctors
* women's aid workers

This is not an exhaustive list. You may be able to think of other groups and agencies in your neighbourhood!

We've been reluctant to do any more with the local health and social service people ever since we got together to set up a food co-op. We agreed to house it in our building because we were the only place that had room. Although they were all eager to help at first, they soon withdrew once it got going. We were left to run it and now find ourselves having to do all the work to get some funding to keep it going until it can run by itself. It takes up a lot of our time – we only carry on because local people find it so useful.

(a voluntary project worker)

Some Potential Problems

It is easy to see collaboration and partnership through rose-tinted spectacles; as the panacea to the difficulties associated with working on family poverty issues. But they can be areas of conflict. Collaboration and partnership bring with them their own set of tensions and difficulties that need to be recognised and worked through before their benefits can be experienced. Some of the potential problems are listed below.

* The interests of agencies and groups do not necessarily coincide: there can be conflicts of interests between agencies and groups with different objectives.
* Collaborative projects can be difficult to maintain: they require time and effort and may demand the development of new skills.
* Collaborative work tends to be seen as low priority when resources are stretched.
* It can result in more referrals: this may cause problems for individual agencies and groups if not anticipated.
* What starts off as a collaborative initiative can end up in the lap of a single agency or group, who may be left to staff and fund the initiative in the long run. This not only defeats the object of collaborative initiatives but can also lead to ill feeling between agencies and groups.

Some Starting Points for Collaborative Work

* **If conterminous boundaries do not exist between agencies, try to promote them.** The development of conterminous boundaries will increase the likelihood of effective collaborative work, but need to be developed at area or departmental level rather than neighbourhood level. If you do not have conterminous boundaries with other agencies, you should be informing (or reminding) senior management of the difficulties it creates and encouraging other agencies to do the same.

* **Do not see inter-agency work as something separate from or as an alternative to working with local residents.** Integrated approaches will be meaningless unless they are concerned with the issues that members of the community identify as important.

* **Try to develop a team policy to underpin collaborative work.** Close proximity and frequent contact with other agencies and groups alone will not produce integrated working or collaboration. Your team needs to have collaborative work as an integral part of its action plan. Collaboration should be part of the brief of all team members. It needs to be seen as a

legitimate priority and not a secondary activity.

- **Find out about the roles and work of other agencies.** Misconceptions about other agencies are the most common cause of conflict between agencies. Could team members spend a day with other teams to find out about their work? Could you invite another team to come and share information about roles and areas of commonality and difference?

- **Identify the extent of the team's freedom to collaborate and integrate plans at neighbourhood level.** Agency policies may determine the boundaries of formal collaboration with other teams. However, even when the opportunities for formal collaboration may be limited, numerous opportunities remain to collaborate informally, particularly at the level of work with individual families or local groups.

- **Consider developing formal liaison machinery.** Effective formal networks for communication are crucial. Could your individual team members carry out liaison roles with other agencies and support or create workers' forums? Try working with other agencies and residents to identify a formal network for communication between community groups, voluntary projects, workers' groups and agency heads.

- **Try to develop regular, face to face contact with other agencies and groups.** Do not always communicate by phone. Develop regular discussion and co-operation over day-to-day casework – do not use contacts solely to make referrals.

- **Try to oil the wheels of relationships with other agencies and groups.** Offer something to other agencies and groups as well as taking from them.

- **Identify the skills that you need to carry out collaborative work.** Many traditional training courses do not pay a lot of attention to this work, yet the skills required are often very different from skills needed to work with families. You could try some joint skills training with other agencies.

We – that's myself, a health visitor and a community worker – had been meeting to share our concerns about the number of women in the neighbourhood who said they were very stressed, some of whom were on tranquillisers. It is hardly surprising they felt so stressed – many of them were bringing up their kids in overcrowded and damp homes with little support and no money. We decided to arrange and put on two afternoon training sessions for workers – one on tranquilliser abuse and the other on stress management. The local Tranx Support Group has its own worker. She ran the sessions with a member of the Tranx group. Both sessions were well attended. We had workers from education, health, social services, the community centre and the local vicar and everyone said they found the sessions useful. It certainly raised people's awareness of the issues and people seemed to find the relaxation useful themselves! Following the sessions some of us got together to see what we could do to help stressed women and to help them to avoid the need to take tranquillisers. So far we have been able to set up and run a stress management group, which is co-worked by me and a health visitor, and a group to offer support to parents. It's been really useful working with other agency workers. It's given me a different perspective on stress and the support that families need.

(A social worker, talking about her work with other agency workers)

! Team activity 6A will help you to identify other agencies and groups to work with on family poverty issues.

Information Sheet

TRANSLATING TEAM STRATEGIES INTO INDIVIDUAL PRACTICE

Workers respond to issues in a variety of ways. This team training handbook is concerned with team responses to poverty in the belief that family support strategies will be most effective if agency teams have a co-ordinated response, and are working towards common goals, with complementary methods of practice. Team responses, however, require that individual team members think about what team strategies and goals mean for them. This information sheet identifies some guidelines that will help you, as individuals within a team, to translate team responses into individual work.

Translating Team to Individual

Unless individuals are able to translate what team strategies and perspectives mean for their own work, team approaches can become fragmented. Team goals and strategies need to be incorporated into individual action plans. It is important to acknowledge that this process is an active process that needs to be carefully thought out. Below is a list of some of the things which may help you to do this.

Key points for individuals:

* Try to identify at the beginning of each week what the team's goals mean for your work as an individual within the team: be specific about the tasks involved;

* Identify each week whether you need to change what you do, how you do it, and who you work with;

* If you are finding it difficult to work out how you fit in, raise your concerns in team meetings and individual supervision sessions;

* Ensure that you have an opportunity to talk to your team leader or manager about your training needs or any difficulties you may be having. You may be able to use an appraisal procedure to do this.

Key points for the team:

* Encourage openness within the team: individuals need to feel that it is okay to express difficulties;

* Do not isolate individuals who are experiencing difficulties or appear resistant;

* Establish where there is common ground between team members;

* Openly acknowledge that it is normal to experience feelings of conflict;

* Identify and plan to deal with actual conflict and competing demands;

* Be patient: do not push people to make very rapid changes if they feel threatened;

* Consider introducing peer group support: team members can pair up to provide support and feedback on each other's work. For example, a team member could invite her/his peer to sit in on a group work session or a visit to a family (with the permission of the group or family) to give feedback on performance.

Key points for team leaders/managers:

* Check whether supervision arrangements are adequate to provide support for individuals who may be experiencing difficulties;

* Encourage individuals in team meetings and individual supervision sessions to see their own work in relation to the overall work of the team and raise any difficulties they are having;

* Identify the training and staff development needs of individual team

members. These may be different from the team's needs as a whole;

*   Try holding team supervision sessions which include planning and evaluation, and deal with difficulties and conflicts.

! Team activity 6C is designed to help you to work out what changes you need to make to your individual practice and work out your support needs. Team activity 6D will help your team to identify any training needs.

Summary and Conclusion

This section has been concerned with the process of engaging with families and other workers. The team activities have encouraged you to think about how you work with families. Building responsive and effective services for families is not only dependent on what you do but how you do it. The methods you use need to be clearly linked to what you are trying to achieve.

This section also encouraged you to look at the value of collaboration and to think about how you can extend your contacts with other agencies and groups. Collaboration needs to be a core element of work in the area of family poverty. Some of the main criticisms from families relate to the failure of the health and welfare community to make co-ordinated responses to their needs.

Co-ordinated responses also need to come from single agency teams, with team planning acting as a major vehicle to ensure that this happens. However, team plans can only materialise if team strategies are translated into individual practice. This section has encouraged you to think about what team plans mean for your individual practice with families in poverty and to identify your training and support needs.

BUILDING AN EVALUATION PLAN

Introduction

This section examines the remaining stage in the process of building responsive strategies for families in poverty: the evaluation stage. Although this team training handbook deals with the evaluation stage in the last section, this does not signify that it is the final stage in the process! If you look back to the flow chart on page 4 you will see that evaluation is part of the cyclical process of assessing, setting goals and objectives and responding. It is a continuous part of a dynamic process. This section looks at the value, purpose and process of evaluating fieldwork practice.

Aims of the Section

i)   to identify the purpose and value of evaluation;

ii) to enable workers to work out how they will evaluate practice.

Team Activities

- 7A   Planning an evaluation programme
- 7B   Evaluating the programme in the handbook

Information Sheet

- Evaluating practice

Notes for Facilitator

- Ensure that your team does complete this section! It is a key section, and essential in ensuring the effectiveness of fieldwork strategies.
- Emphasise the need to build realistic evaluation plans so that people do not become demoralised if they cannot carry through their plans.
- Make sure you sell the positive aspects. Consider reading some of the texts on evaluation identified in section 8 to prepare you for this role.
- If the team has difficulties planning their evaluation, you could ask them whether you would all benefit from the help of someone from outside the team who is experienced in evaluation, for example, someone from another team or agency, or someone from your training division.

Team Activity 🅐

PLANNING AN EVALUATION PROGRAMME

Estimated time: 2 hours
Method: brain-storm, group discussion
Materials: flip chart, pens, copies of team action plan, copies of the Evaluation Plan
(page 110)

Relevant information sheet: *Evaluating practice*

This team activity will help your team to work out a programme of evaluation for your team action plan. Using a copy of your team action plan, work through the tasks below to decide on an evaluation programme.

1 **As a group, brain-storm to make a list of all the reasons why evaluation will help you in your practice. Ask your facilitator to write your list on the flip chart. Pin it up on the wall to remind you of the positive things about evaluation. Use it to remind yourselves of all the reasons why you should evaluate!** (10 mins)

2 **As a group, look at the copy of your team action plan. Use a copy of the Evaluation Plan for each goal. Take the first goal and set of objectives only and write them on a copy of the Evaluation Plan.**

3 **For the first goal and set of objectives:** (60 – 90 mins)

   i) Decide how the success of each objective can be realistically measured. Identify a method or methods for each objective in column 1.

   ii) Identify at what point/s evaluation procedures need to be carried out (for example, continuous monitoring, administration of a questionnaire in the middle/at end of programme, weekly feedback at the end of a group session). Write this in column 2.

   iii) Identify any procedure for collecting information that needs to be set up (for example, record how many people attend a new group, drop-in session, welfare rights session etc on index cards). Identify this in column 3.

   iv) Identify which members of the team will be responsible for which parts of the evaluation and discuss what changes, if any, need to be made to work allocations for the evaluation to happen. Write this in column 4.

   v) Check out that all concerned feel that they have the skills to carry out the part of the evaluation that they are responsible for. If they do not, decide whether someone else can help with it or whether the evaluation should be postponed until the person/s have undergone some evaluation skills training.

   vi) Identify areas where the whole team needs support and/or training, and try to identify who could offer this – team members, workers in other agencies, your training department or your information and research department?

Ask your facilitator to write up the main points of your discussion on a flip chart as they are raised.

4 **Decide whether you need any additional resources to carry out this evaluation. Identify whether these resources are available or whether you need to ask your manager for more resources. If resources are not available, will you abandon your evaluation plan or adjust it to the resources you have?** (30 mins)

Action Points!

* Ask your facilitator to write up the main points from your discussions and give each member of the team a copy.

* Keep a copy of the evaluation plan with your main team action plan. Everyone should have a copy of each.

* Make a date to devise an evaluation plan for your other goals. You may wish to see how you get on evaluating your first goal before you do this but remember that if you delay, you may not be able to collect all the information you need to evaluate other goals.

EVALUATION PLAN
(use with activity 7A)

Goal:

Objectives	1 Evaluation methods	2 Evaluation points	3 Information collection procedure	4 Person/s responsible

Team Activity 7B

EVALUATING THE PROGRAMME IN THE HANDBOOK

Estimated time: 1 hour
Method: individual work and group discussion
Materials: copies of this activity sheet for each team member

You have now worked through a programme of learning and planning around family poverty. This is the last activity in the team training handbook and it aims to help you to evaluate this programme. Your evaluation will also be of use to the Health Promotion in Poverty Project, from which this team training handbook evolved. When you have completed this evaluation, we would be grateful if you would send us a copy of this evaluation sheet. This will help us to evaluate the effectiveness of the materials.

1   **Working individually and using a sheet each, try to answer the following questions:**
    (15 mins)

    i)   What were the most useful or positive aspects of the programme?

    ii)   What were the least helpful aspects of the programme?

    iii) What was the most difficult aspect of the programme?

    iv)   What were the three most useful things that you personally got out of the programme?

    v)   What did you think of the structure of the team training handbook?

    vi)   Which activities did you find most helpful?

    vii) Which activities did you find least helpful?

2   **As a team group share your thoughts and feelings about the programme. Some other things you might like to discuss and would be useful feedback for the project are:** (45 mins)

    i)   Did you find learning and planning as a team useful? If so why?

SECTION 7

ii) Did it have any advantages over other types of training you have been involved in? If so, what were they?

iii) Which other current/future training needs could usefully be met using this method of team training?

We would be grateful if you would give us some information about yourself:

1   What is your job title?

2   Which agency do you work for (health visiting service, community education etc)?

3   Did you use these materials as part of a team? If not, how did you use them?

4   Please add any further comments that you think we would find helpful below:

Please send a copy of this evaluation to:
The Health Promotion in Poverty Project
Department of Applied Social Studies
University of Warwick
Coventry, CV4 7AL

Information Sheet

EVALUATING PRACTICE

This information sheet attempts to demystify the process of evaluation and encourage you to see its positive value. It aims to give your team a brief introduction to evaluating practice. It offers some guidelines that will enable you to take the first step in building an evaluative element into your team action plan.

What is Evaluation?

* It is an assessment of what has been achieved in practice against what was intended, that is whether you have attained the goals you set for practice and if so, how;

* It is a process that helps you to plan for the future: the knowledge you gain from evaluation can help you to reformulate goals and build more effective action plans.

> **Evaluation is about measuring the attainment of goals and the suitability of methods. This means that it cannot take place unless you have specified a clear set of goals in the first place!**

Why Evaluate Practice?

* It is necessary to assess the effectiveness of past work to see if it has been successful and should be repeated;

* Information is needed to plan future work;

* It aids the identification of 'good practice';

* It helps to justify expenditure and gain further resources, especially when resources are scarce;

* It helps to focus practice by being clear and specific about what one is trying to achieve;

* Fieldworkers need to be accountable: to themselves, clients, colleagues and employers or funders. Evaluation is a way of being accountable.[1]

> **Evaluation is the only consistent way to learn whether on balance, your fieldwork strategies and responses to family poverty are positive and achieving what was intended.[2]**

Types of Evaluation

There are two broad types of evaluation:

* **outcome evaluation:** measuring what was achieved;

* **process evaluation:** measuring the appropriateness of the methods used and trying to explain why certain outcomes occurred.

Different people are likely to want different types of evaluation. For example, budget holders or project funders may only be interested in outcome evaluation. However, people who are interested in the consequences of practice for families may be more interested in process evaluation.

> **When evaluation is part of the dynamic process of building fieldwork strategies it needs to be concerned with both outcomes and process.**

The discovery of a particular outcome is of limited value unless the factors and conditions that caused the outcome are known. If only the outcome is known, then it will be difficult to reproduce the same effect again.

When is a Good Time to Evaluate?

Evaluation can start at any time. Never use the excuse 'it's too late' to put off evaluation.

Even if you cannot do anything else, you can take a reflective look back and ask some critical questions of what you have been doing and what you may or may not have achieved.

But the timing of evaluation does have consequences for the amount and type of information that you can collect.[3] Ideally it should start with planning and continue throughout the piece of work. For example if you wished to evaluate whether changing clinic times, duty hours or drop-in times increased users' accessibility to the team, it would be necessary to do a 'before and after' study to see if more people used the service. If you did not plan the evaluation until the new programme had been operating for some time you would have missed out on the 'before' information. Leaving evaluation to the end of a project or initiative rules out the opportunity to use the information to improve the project while it is in progress.

> **Good practice evaluation starts when the project or intervention starts and uses the information at all stages to reformulate goals, objectives, methods and timescales.**

Carrying Out Evaluation

Different goals and objectives will need to be evaluated in different ways. Some will need to be evaluated using quantitative methods and others will need to be evaluated by qualitative methods.

- **Quantitative methods:** are used to measure quantity (how many people? who? how many times? when? etc.). They use numbers and statistical information and are useful in outcome evaluation;

- **Qualitative methods:** are about measuring quality (how good was it? was it what people wanted? etc.). They are based on words and descriptions and useful in process evaluation.

An Example of Evaluating a Goal

The following example looks at how one goal and set of objectives could be evaluated using both methods.

Goal: to increase take-up of benefits among Black and minority ethnic families

Objective i): to make contact with and offer welfare benefits advice to Black and minority ethnic groups;

Possible quantitative method: counting and recording how many groups were contacted and how many took up the offer of advice.

Possible qualitative method: using a questionnaire, group discussion or individual interviews with participants to find out what they found useful/not useful about the session.

Objective ii): to set up a meeting with other agency workers to raise their awareness of low take-up of benefits among Black and minority ethnic families;

Possible quantitative method: identifying whether the meeting took place, administering a questionnaire before and some weeks after the meeting to see if and how levels of awareness had altered, and what effect these had on practice.

Possible qualitative method: identifying how successful the meeting was by asking participants at the end of it whether they found it useful to discuss the issue with you. The example given above illustrates two points:

i) *Each objective can be measured in a variety of ways.* The number of ways in which you evaluate each objective will depend on what is realistic within the restraints of time. From the example above it is possible to see that some of the methods were very easy and quick to carry out and only took a little forethought and planning.

ii) *It is necessary to set up procedures to collect and record information before the evaluation starts.* In the example above it is clear that there would need to be a way of recording the number of groups contacted to discuss up-take of benefits. If this was not in place before the programme started then valuable information would be lost.

Some Guidelines for Practice

There are five key stages to evaluating practice. Follow these key stages to plan and carry out your own evaluations:

Stage 1: Examine the goals and objectives in your team action plan. Decide which objectives can be evaluated using which indices, methods and measurement techniques and at what stage in the programme.

Stage 2: Incorporate the evaluation plan into your action plan. Decide who will do what and when, and set up any recording procedures that will be needed. Check out that the plan is acceptable to all concerned.

Stage 3: Carry out the evaluation and collect the required information.

Stage 4: Analyse and interpret it.

Stage 5: Use it! Primarily, use it to reformulate your action plan. Check to see if your goals, objectives, methods and timescales need to change. If they do, change them. But your evaluation can have other uses. Write it up and circulate your results to colleagues, other agencies and recipients of services. Other people can benefit from your successes and failures.

Some examples of quantitative and qualitative methods

Quantitative
Surveys and questionnaires (which facilitate counting or categorising), observations, referral/caseload analysis, analysis of agency data, costing studies.

Qualitative
Interviews and questionnaires (such as consumer satisfaction surveys which give feedback on quality of services), case reviews, peer- and self-evaluation, analysis of case studies, group evaluation.

! Team activity 7A will help you to plan an evaluation programme that you can use with your action plan.

SECTION 7

115

Summary and Conclusion

This section has looked at the purpose, value and stages of evaluating practice in the area of family poverty. Evaluation needs to be an integral part of everyday work. Remember that neither your team action plan nor your evaluation plan are set in tablets of stone. They will need to be continually up-dated as circumstances change. It is critically important to ensure that action planning and responding are seen as part of a cyclical process. Each stage in the process contributes to and is amended, in turn, by the stages that follow. Although you now may have worked through this team training handbook you should not consider that you have reached the end. In reality, it is only the beginning. You will find that it will be useful to return to some of the exercises from time to time to focus your thinking.

Family poverty seems likely to continue. Even though you may feel that the opportunities for radical change are limited or that you are only responding at the edges of poverty, remember that what you do, no matter how small, can have considerable benefits for families. Evaluating how consumers feel about your actions will help you to maintain motivation and a commitment to work on family poverty issues.

References

1   Combes, G. (1990). 'Evaluating family education'. *Journal of Community Education,* Vol. 8, No. 4.

2   Graessle, L., Kingsley, S. (1986). *Measuring Change, Making Changes: An Approach to Evaluation.* London, London Community Health Resource.

3   Graessle, L., Kingsley, S. (1986). ibid.

SOURCES OF FURTHER INFORMATION AND SUGGESTIONS FOR FURTHER READING

Sources of Further Information

Action on Benefits, 124–130 Southwark Street, London, SE1

Benefits Research Unit, Department of Social Policy, University of Nottingham, Nottingham, NG7 2RD

British Association of Social Workers, 16 Kent Street, Birmingham, B5.

British Medical Association, Tavistock Square, London, WC1H 9JR.

Child Poverty Action Group, 1–5 Bath Street, London EC2

Church Action on Poverty, 27 Blackfriars Road, Salford, Greater Manchester.

Commission for Racial Equality, 10–12 Allington Street, London, SW1.

Equal Opportunities Commission, Quay Street, Manchester, M3.

Family Policy Studies Centre, 231 Baker Street, London, NW1.

Health Education Authority, Hamilton House, Mabledon Place, London, WC1.

Health Visitors' Association, 50 Southwark Street, London, SE1

London Food Commission, 88 Old Street, London, EC1.

Low Pay Unit, 9 Upper Berkeley Street, London, EC1.

Maternity Alliance, 15 Britannia Street, London, NW1.

National Council for One Parent Families 255 Kentish Town Road, London, NW5.

National Council For Voluntary Organisations, 26 Bedford Square, London, WC1.

Policy Studies Institute, 100 Park Village East, London, NW1.

Shelter, 157 Waterloo Road, London, SE1.

Women's Health Information Centre, 52 Featherstone Street, London EC1

Suggestions for Further Reading

INTRODUCTION AND SECTION 1
Satow, A., Evans, M. (1983). *Working with Groups.* London, Health Education Council/Tacade.

SECTION 2
Definitions of poverty:
Blackburn, C. (1991). *Poverty and Health: Working with Families.* Buckingham, Open University Press. Chapter 1.

Oppenheim, C. (1990). *Poverty: The Facts.* London, Child Poverty Action Group.

Definitions and perceptions of poverty and fieldwork practice:
Becker, S. (1988). 'Poverty Awareness' in Becker, S., MacPherson, S. (eds) *Public Issues, Private Pain.* London, Social Services Insight.

Popay, J., Dhooge, Y., Shipman, C. (1986). *Unemployment and Health: What Role for Health and Social Services?* Research Report, No. 3. London, Health Education Council.

Silburn, R. (1988). 'Definitions, meanings and experiences of poverty: a framework' in Becker, S., MacPherson, S. (eds) *Public Issues, Private Pain.* London, Social Services Insight.

SECTION 8

117

Measuring poverty:

Blackburn, C. (1991). *Poverty and Health: Working with Families.* Buckingham, Open University Press. Chapter 1.

Oppenheim, C. (1990). *Poverty: The Facts.* London, Child Poverty Action Group.

Poverty levels and distribution between social groups:

Blackburn, C. (1991). *Poverty and Health: Working with Families.* Buckingham, Open University Press. Chapter 1.

Oppenheim, C. (1990). *Poverty: The Facts.* London, Child Poverty Action Group.

SECTION 3
Experience of poverty:

Blackburn, C. (1991). *Poverty and Health: Working with Families.* Buckingham, Open University Press. Chapter 1.

Bradshaw, J., Holmes, H. (1989). *Living on the Edge.* London, Child Poverty Action Group.

Burghes, L. (1980). *Living from Hand to Mouth.* London, Family Services Unit/Child Poverty Action Group.

Glendenning, C., Millar, J. (eds) (1987). *Women in Poverty in Britain.* Wheatsheaf, Brighton.

Harrison, P. (1983). *Inside the Inner City: Life Under the Cutting Edge.* Harmondsworth, Penguin.

Mack, J., Lansley, S. (1985). *Poor Britain.* London, Allen and Unwin.

MacPherson, S. (1988). 'Getting by and getting through' in Becker, S., MacPherson, S. (eds) *Public Issues, Private Pain.* London, Social Services Insight.

Oppenheim, C. (1990). *Poverty: The Facts.* London, Child Poverty Action Group.

Housing, fuel poverty and health:

Blackburn, C. (1991). *Poverty and Health: Working with Families.* Buckingham, Open University Press. Chapter 4.

Conway, J. (ed.) (1988). *Prescription for Poor Health: The Crisis for Homeless Families.* London Food Commission; Maternity Alliance; SHAC; Shelter.

Luthera, M. (1989). 'Race, community, housing and the state – a historical overview' in Bhat, A. *et al, Britain's Black Population,* 2nd edition. Aldershot, Gower.

Morris, J. (1988). 'Keeping women in their place'. *Roof,* July/August: 21–22.

Stearn, J. (1986). 'An expensive way of making children ill'. *Roof,* September/October: 12–14.

Poverty and health:

Blackburn, C. (1991). *Poverty and Health: Working with Families.* Buckingham, Open University Press. Chapters 2 and 5.

Blaxter, M. (1990). *Health and Lifestyles.* London, Routledge.

British Medical Association (1987). *Deprivation and Ill Health.* London, British Medical Association.

Whitehead, M. (1987). *The Health Divide.* London, Health Education Council.

Food Poverty:

Blackburn, C. (1991). *Poverty and Health: Working with Families.* Buckingham, Open University Press. Chapter 3.

Cole-Hamilton, I., Lang, T. (1985). *Tightening Belts: A Report of the Impact of Poverty on Food.* London, London Food Commission.

Graham, H. (1987). 'Women's poverty and caring' in Glendenning, C., Millar, J. (eds) *Women and Poverty in Britain.* Brighton, Wheatsheaf.

SECTION 4

Building up poverty profiles:

Dauncy, J. *et al.* (1990). *Health Profiling.* London, Health Visitors' Association.

Henderson, P., Thomas, D. (1980). *Skills in Neighbourhood Work.* National Institute for Social Work. London, Allen and Unwin. Chapter 3.

Dhooge, Y., Becker, S. (1989). *Working with Unemployment and Poverty: A Training Manual for Social Services.* Department of Social Sciences, South Bank Polytechnic.

SECTION 5

Blackburn, C. (1991). *Poverty and Health: Working with Families.* Buckingham, Open University Press. Chapter 7.

Dhooge, Y., Becker, S. (1989). *Working with Unemployment and Poverty: A Training Manual for Social Services.* Department of Social Sciences, South Bank Polytechnic.

Hadley, R. *et al.* (1987). *A Community Social Worker's Handbook.* London, Tavistock Publications.

Henderson, P., Thomas, D. (1980). *Skills in Neighbourhood Work.* National Institute for Social Work. London, Allen and Unwin. Chapter 4.

Luker, K., Orr, J. (1985). *Health Visiting.* Oxford, Blackwell Scientific Publications. Chapter 2.

Smale, G. *et al.* (1988). *Community Social Work: A Paradigm for Change.* London, National Institute for Social Work.

Commentaries and guides to the Children Act (1989):

University of Leicester, School of Social Work and Faculty of Law (1991). *Children in Need and their Families: A Manual for Managers on Part III of the Children Act (1989).* University of Leicester/Department of Health.

Armstrong, H. *et al.* (1990). *Working with the Children Act 1989: An Introduction for Practitioners in Education, Health and Social Work.* London, National Children's Bureau.

SECTION 6

Dhooge, Y., Becker, S. (1989). *Working with Unemployment and Poverty: A Training Manual for Social Services.* Department of Social Sciences, South Bank Polytechnic.

Hadley, R. *et al.* (1987). *A Community Social Worker's Handbook.* London, Tavistock Publications.

Hardiker, P., Barker, M. (1988). 'A window on childcare, poverty and social work' in Becker, S., MacPherson, S. (eds) *Public Issues, Private Pain.* London, Social Services Insight.

Popay, J., Dhooge, Y., Shipman, C. (1986). *Unemployment and Health: What Role for Health and Social Services?* Research Report, No. 3. London, Health Education Council.

Slipman, S. (1988). 'One parent families: strategies for hope and their implications for help agencies' in Becker, S., MacPherson, S. (eds) *Public Issues, Private Pain.* London, Social Services Insight.

Smale, G. *et al.* (1988). *Community Social Work: A Paradigm for Change.* London, National Institute for Social Work.

SECTION 7

David, S. *et al.* (1988). 'Evaluation and Community Social Work'. *Practice,* Vol. 2, No. 3, 256–68.

Graessle, L. and Kingsley, S. (1986). *Measuring Change, Making Changes: An Approach to Evaluation.* London, National Community Health Resource.

Preston-Shoot, M., Williams, J. (1987). 'Evaluting the effectiveness of practice' *Practice,* Vol. 1, No. 4, 393–405.